2009: The Best
Women's Stage Monologues and Scenes

Edited and with a Foreword
by Lawrence Harbison

MONOLOGUE AND SCENE STUDY SERIES

A SMITH AND KRAUS BOOK

Published by Smith and Kraus, Inc.
177 Lyme Road, Hanover, NH 03755
SmithandKraus.com

First Edition:October 2009
10 9 8 7 6 5 4 3 2 1

Cover design by Dan Mehling, dmehling@gmail.com
Text design by Julia Hill Gignoux, Freedom Hill Design and Book Production

The Scene Study Series 1067-3253
ISBN-13 978-1-57525-761-7 / ISBN-10 1-57525-761-0
Library of Congress Control Number: 2009936731

To receive prepublication information about upcoming Smith and Kraus books, news of special promotions and private sales, join our eNewsletter at smithandkraus.com. To order, visit us at smithandkraus.com or call toll-free (888) 282-2881. Look for our books in all fine bookstores.

CONTENTS

Foreword

This year Smith and Kraus has decided to combine its annual best monologues and best scenes anthologies. The scenes included in this book are either for two women or for one man and one woman. The latter are scenes in which the female role is predominant.

Here you will find a rich and varied selection of monologues and scenes from plays that were produced and/or published in the 2008–2009 theatrical season. Most are for younger performers (teens through thirties), but there are also some excellent pieces for women in their forties and fifties, and even a few for older performers. Some are comic (laughs), some are dramatic (generally, no laughs). Some are rather short, some are rather long. All represent the best in contemporary playwriting.

Several of the monologues are by playwrights whose work may be familiar to you, such as Don Nigro, Sam Bobrick, Adam Rapp, Bill Cain, José Rivera, Stephen Belber, Keith Reddin, Naomi Iizuka, Michael Weller, Roberto Aguirre-Sacasa, Richard Vetere, and Nicky Silver; others are by exciting up-and-comers like Steven Leigh Morris, Saviana Stanescu, Liz Flahive, Stephanie Allison Walker, Cheri Magid, Jennifer Maisel, Andrew Grosso, David Caudle, Nina Raine, John Kolvenbach, Sylvia Reed, and Lucy Thurber. The scenes are by master playwrights, such as Rivera, Gina Gionfriddo, Jeffrey Hatcher, A. R. Gurney, and Aguirre-Sacasa, and by exciting new playwrights, such as Vincent Delaney, Stanescu, Lydia Stryk, Grosso, and Larry Kunofsky.

Most of the plays from which these monologues have been culled have been published and, hence, are readily available either from the publisher/licensor or from a theatrical bookstore such as Drama Book Shop in New York. A few plays may not be published for a while, in which case contact the author or his or her agent to request a copy of the entire text of the play containing the monologue that suits your fancy. Information on publishers/rights holders may be found in the rights and permissions section in the back of this anthology.

Break a leg in that audition! Knock 'em dead in class!

Lawrence Harbison
Brooklyn, New York

MONOLOGUES

ALIENS WITH EXTRAORDINARY SKILLS
Saviana Stanescu

Dramatic
Nadia, twenties

> *Nadia is an illegal immigrant from Moldova, here describing being abused at a party in Soho, New York City, where she was providing "the entertainment." She is talking to the imaginary immigration officers INS 1 and INS 2 who haunt her and are trying to deport her.*

NADIA: Let me explain . . . I get there . . . I am soooo excited . . . My heart is pumping hot steams not blood . . . This guy Mike ushers me in. He is confident, elegant. He says: "Hi, pretty lady." He takes my arm. He introduces me to people. He tells them: "She's from the former Soviet Union." He prepares a drink for me. A cocktail. A Cosmo! Yeah . . . I drink, I smoke, like everybody else . . . I am cool . . . I dance for him, for them . . . I am sexy, I shake it well . . . A few hours pass, I think I get tired . . . My stomach is a bit upset . . . But it doesn't matter, everything is too perfect. I walk into this room . . . Beautiful room . . . A bedroom with red-painted walls and huge windows . . . I can see the Hudson River . . . great view! . . . Red lights dancing on the river . . . like mouths with blood-red lips . . . I press my face on that window . . . My feet hurt from dancing two hours on spike heels . . . I take off my shoes for a moment. Just for a moment. I think I'm alone. I am not alone. Mike enters. He comes closer . . . I can smell his expensive aftershave . . . He's gonna kiss me. No. He puts his hand under my skirt . . . Strange . . . His face looks different . . . "Say something in Russian, Natasha!" He keeps calling me Natasha . . . "You Russian babes are all so fucking sexy." . . . What is he doing? . . . His hand . . . His fingers . . . Pushing my underwear, pushing . . . "C'mon, Natasha. Say FUCK ME, Mike, in Russian, Natasha!" . . . *(Pause.)* I had to run barefoot out of that room. Out of that apartment. Out . . . and I left them there — I left my shoes . . . I didn't have time to grab my Manolo Blahniks . . . Lupita will kill me and that's fine with me . . . that's fine . . . I deserve that.

ALOHA SAY THE PRETTY GIRLS
Naomi Iizuka

Seriocomic
Vivian, late twenties

> *Vivian's life is coming apart. When the play begins, her boyfriend of many years announces that he's leaving her. What nobody knows, including her now ex-boyfriend, is that she's pregnant. Vivian keeps this information to herself until she can't anymore. Here, she's a substitute teacher for a kindergarten class. She tells the children about her pregnancy in this aria of anxiety.*

> *(Vivian clutches a suitcase, a plant, and a large map of the United States. She can't carry everything. She puts down the suitcase and the plant.)*

VIVIAN: hello. i'm your substitute teacher, sort of. your real teacher, myrna, she's gone away for a little while, so she asked me to cover for her even though i'm not sure it's legal, because i'm not technically a teacher, and i don't know what i'm supposed to be doing exactly, which is how i feel often these days, not just here. anyway i can't stay that long. i didn't know what to say to you guys, so i brought this map, this is a map of the continental united states. right now, we're here. this is new york. i'm leaving new york. i'm flying all the way across all these states, and i'm ending up here in california, and after california, there's nothing but ocean as far as the eye can see, and then the next real land mass you get to is hawaii, i guess, which really, if you think about it, is just a few tiny islands in the middle of this huge, enormous ocean, in the middle of nowhere, so tiny you can barely see them, and they're so far away. i mean, it's a whole different map that i didn't happen to bring with me today, maybe not even a map, maybe more of a globe, which i don't have, i have no globe, and anyway, it's not like i'm even going to hawaii, because where i'm going is here: california. i wasn't really planning on going to california, but i have this friend, i don't know if "friend" is the right word, he's kind of a friend, i mean, he was a friend once, but to be honest, i don't know exactly how i feel about him, because i think we're actually very different people, and i'm not sure we communicate very well, and i'm not sure we have all that much in common anymore, but "friend," i guess, is the only word out there, and so my friend, what he did, which was really a very kind thing and something that a friend would, in fact, do, he got me a job working for him, doing something, i'm not sure what, but it doesn't even really matter, because it's a job, and it's a whole new beginning for me, and that sounds really good right this second, because the thing is, i really need something like that in my life right now, because i'm finding i have this need lately to feel settled and safe and sane, which it feels more and more like i never am here, i'm not sure why, because the thing is, i just found out a little while ago that i'm going to have a baby. wow. that was weird. that just came out. you're the first people i've told. i was going to tell will, but then things got strange, and one thing led to another, and anyway, you don't know will, i'm not sure i know will. i don't know why i'm telling you all this. i don't know you, and maybe it's not appropriate to talk about this kind of stuff with small children, but for some reason, i don't know why, i feel really at ease with you. you all seem very wise for your years. i'm not ready for all of this, but it's not really about me anymore, because the thing is it's not just me floating around in space now. it's also this little person inside of me, who's also kinda floating around in space, and who probably looks kinda like a little fishy right about now, and that is so scary to me, but it's also kind of amazing. you were all little fishies once. and all of you have mommies and daddies, too. well, my baby doesn't have a daddy, which is a little complicated and strange and not how i wanted it to be or thought it would be. but you know what? it's ok. i mean, there was a daddy once, but he fell in love with somebody else, and then after that, he kinda disappeared. we think he maybe got eaten by a giant animal or maybe he was abducted by aliens. nobody knows for sure. it's a mystery. this all happened here in new york, in brooklyn actually, which is right about here. i like maps so much. i like how everything is pink and orange and aquamarine, and all the countries and states look like little funny-shaped candies. i like how all the names of the places are written in these perfect, block letters. i like that maps tell you where you are, and how to get to where you're going. but the thing about a map, the best thing of all, you look at it, and places that are really big and faraway, don't seem so big and faraway. a whole continent is the distance from your thumb to your fingertip. a whole entire ocean is as big as the palm of your hand. magic. truly. well, i guess that's all i have to say for now. it was very nice being your substitute teacher. you were very good today, and i hope you all eventually grow up to be happy and productive people in the world. i guess it's recess now. good-bye.

ALOHA SAY THE PRETTY GIRLS
Naomi Iizuka

Dramatic
Wendy, late twenties

> *Wendy is a frustrated actress who has left New York and ended up in
> Hawaii as a hula dancer. Her girlfriend Joy wants to be in a commit-
> ted relationship with her, but Wendy has a horror of being in a com-
> mitted relationship with anyone. This monologue occurs after Wendy
> and Joy have had a fight during which Joy told Wendy she loves her but
> Wendy rejected her.*

WENDY: why? i mean, why is it that all of a sudden everybody you know starts
wanting to get married and have babies, and everything that comes
along with getting married and having babies? is it just some kinda instinct, some kinda lizard brain instinct, like turtles or lemmings or
moose in spring, or is it maybe this sudden awareness that kicks in that
you're not getting any younger, and someday you're maybe gonna get
sick and old and then maybe you're gonna die — well, not maybe, you
are, i mean you are gonna die, we're all gonna die, that's the deal — but
whatever, maybe you're having trouble with that concept, or maybe you
just don't want to be doing all of that stuff alone, and think you can
think of this in terms of musical chairs, i think it's actually a lot like musical chairs, and so there you are, having spent most of your twenties
playing this game of musical chairs, and suddenly it's like you turn
twenty-eight, twenty-nine, and somebody turns the music off, and it
gets really quiet in the room, and you look around, and the thing is,
right, there's not enough chairs to go around, somebody's gonna be left
chairless, somebody's gonna get screwed, and before you know it, everybody's scrambling around, looking for a place to park their ass, and people are getting knocked to the ground, and there's shoving happening,
and elbows in the eyes, and it's ugly, ok, it's really ugly, but you're right
in there, you're in the fray, and so finally, you get yourself a chair, and
you're happy because you're like seated, but then before too long, you
know, you turn to look at the people sitting next to you, and it's like,

who are you again? and what am i doing sitting next to you? do i really want to be sitting next to you? and also, this chair, i'm not so sure about this chair, i mean maybe i don't even want to be seated, maybe i want to stand. . . . so now, ok, this is the thing: i used to fuck guys, and now i fuck girls, and i'm personally very happy about that little change of scenery, but you'd think, you know, that it's a different thing, that this whole musical chair thing, it's a guy/girl thing, and now that i'm doing this girl/girl thing, the whole musical chair thing, it's not going to be the same thing, but it is, it's like the exact same thing, it's like musical chairs only with different chairs.

ALOHA SAY THE PRETTY GIRLS

Naomi Iizuka

Comic
Wendy, late twenties

Wendy is a frustrated actress who has left New York and ended up in Hawaii as a hula dancer. She has a girlfriend, Joy, whom she takes for granted. After she and Joy have a big argument, Joy takes off, and Wendy begins to miss her. This monologue occurs while she's looking for Joy on the beach. She runs into a stranger with a tattoo and shares with him her opinions about tattoos and relationships.

WENDY: joy? joy, is that you? you're not joy. . . . have you, by any chance, seen my girlfriend? her name is joy. i don't know what the hell she's up to. normally, what happens, right, we fight, and she takes off and eventually she comes back, and then we make up, and it's nice for like three minutes, and then we fight, and she takes off, and so it goes, only this time, she's gone, and i don't think she's coming back, and it's kinda throwing me for a loop, and i guess you could say i miss her, i guess i kinda miss her. you know. my skirt is made of grass. i live in a place where people wear skirts made of grass. how did that happen? is that a tattoo? . . . it's very small. it's a very small tattoo. in some cultures, men and women, their whole bodies are tattooed, head to foot, until they're just one big, walking tattoo with a face and some hair. it's a thing . . . oh yeah? well, no offense, but that tattoo is kinda wimpy. that's the tattoo of a man who can't decide, a man who can't commit, a man who dithers. and you know what, you're just too old to be dithering. we're all too old to be dithering. i mean, it's one thing when you're a kid. you can dither all you want as a kid. but as you get older, dithering is really, really unattractive . . . as far as i'm concerned, the tattoo is just the tip of the iceberg. now if you'll excuse me, i need to find joy.

AMERICAN GIRLS
Hilary Bettis

Seriocomic
Katie, fourteen

> *Katie is speaking to her best friend, Amanda, in a deserted bus stop at*
> *one A.M. Katie regrets that she and Amanda went to an amateur con-*
> *test at a strip club and made an audition tape for a man who told them*
> *he was a Hollywood talent scout.*

KATIE: Are you out of your mind??? Sense of adventure? Were you not there
tonight? Were we not doing horrible, disgusting things together tonight?
I have never felt so degraded in my life. I should never have let you talk
me into it. I never thought I would hate you, Amanda, but right now I
hate you more than any person on the face of the earth. Because of you,
I am going to hell. Because of you, everything that I ever worked for in
my whole life is ruined. I love my church. I love Pastor Jim. I love my
parents. My daddy is planning a purity ball for me in two years where I
will pledge my virginity to him until I get married and now I don't know
how I can ever look him in the face again! I don't know how I can ever
go on a date with a decent boy. Ever. Or Rob. How can I ever look at
Rob again? I am a slut. I am nothing more than a little slut. Thank you,
Amanda, thank you so much for making me what I am right now. Just
this afternoon I was a good Christian girl and I loved my life and now
here I am sitting in an old disgusting bus station at one in the morning
with a horrible homeless man and the one person that I thought I could
trust but who turns out to be the most terrible person in the world. You
have totally ruined my life, Amanda. My life is totally ruined. It will
never be the same. Never, ever, ever. I hate you. When we get home, I
want you to clear all your stuff out of my house and I want back everything I ever gave you and I never want to see you again. I will ask Jesus
Christ for forgiveness. And I will pray about it. And I will pray for you
too, Amanda. I will pray that Jesus Christ forgives you for what you did
tonight, and what I did tonight, and what you made me do tonight.

AMERICAN GIRLS
Hilary Bettis

Seriocomic
Amanda, fourteen

*Amanda is speaking to her best friend, Katie, in a deserted bus stop at
one A.M. Katie has just told Amanda that she no longer wants to be her
friend and regrets that she and Amanda danced at an amateur contest
at a strip club and made an audition tape for a man who told them he
was a Hollywood talent scout.*

AMANDA: Can I say something now? I'm sorry if you think that I ruined your
life tonight, Katie, and I'm sorry if you want to blame me for it and
never want to be my best friend again and that hurts me more than you
will ever know because I would give my life for you but you obviously
don't care about that and I'm just disposable like a piece of garbage. You
were my best friend, Katie, and it just makes me sad that you think I'm
a terrible person and that Jesus won't love me anymore and that you have
to pray for me and I wish you wouldn't because I don't want someone
who hates me praying for me. But I just want to tell you something —
Jesus loves us no matter what we do. That's the great thing about Jesus
Christ. Pastor Jim says that to us over and over and over and over again
and everyone seems to understand that except for you because you are
so dramatic and now your life is ruined. I also think you have a very
short memory because you wanted to do this just as much as I did and
in fact it was your idea for me to ask Josh about the fake IDs and you're
the one who always talked about being a star and a celebrity but not the
kind like phony Britney Spears, but the kind like Ashley Tisdale who
loves Jesus so that you could be famous and rich and have a nice house
and a pony that you could ride whenever you wanted and enough
money to donate to Pastor Jim and our church and you would go on talk
shows and you would spread the word of Jesus. This was what you
wanted, Katie, and I, as your best friend, wanted to give that to you anyway that I could. And I thought that we had a good time tonight. I
thought we had the time of our lives. And we met a Hollywood agent
and we did an audition and we may have gotten a little carried away but

I don't think we did anything wrong and even if we did, I know, I know deep deep in my heart, that Jesus will forgive me and that He knows my heart and He knows your heart and He knows that we are good people, Katie, you and me, Katie and Amanda, we are good Christians. Now, doesn't Pastor Jim always say that Jesus will forgive all our transgressions? And if we have transgressed tonight, don't you think Jesus will forgive us? Then I honestly don't know what you are talking about and why you said those hateful things to me and why you are so willing to dump me as a friend, and not just any friend, as a best friend. I really don't understand why all of a sudden you are such a baby. And a bitch.

AMERICAN GIRLS
Hilary Bettis

Seriocomic
Amanda, fourteen

> *Amanda is in her bedroom speaking to a video camera. She is making a tape to put on YouTube. Frank is a supposed Hollywood talent scout whom she and her friend Katie met at an amateur night at a strip club and for whom they made an audition tape.*

AMANDA: Is it on? Hello? Are you on? Oh, OK. So welcome to my boring life. Let's see . . . What has happened . . . Well, school has been out for like almost a month now. I heard from Dana that Kylie has gained like five pounds, and Vanessa is stuck at her grandma's for most of the summer. But Katie and I have been tearing up the town in search of adventure. We went to the pool like almost every day, so now I have an awesome tan and all the men are like in love with us there! And we went camping and we've seen like every movie that has been released in the past several weeks, and we've seen Miley Cyrus's new movie like ten times! And of course church youth group every Wednesday night. That is the best place to get all the latest gossip, plus we get to profess our love for Jesus, which is cool. All in all it has been a pretty good summer so far. We're still waiting for Frank to call us, but Katie says that things in Hollywood take time so we have to be patient. I just wish something big would happen . . . Like an alien landing in a cornfield or something. Sometimes I have this dream that I am walking down the street in this really pretty blue dress, my hair and makeup are perfect, and all the boys are whistling at me. Then all of the sudden Ashley Tisdale and Lindsay Lohan and Jamie-Lynn Spears and Vanessa Hudgens come up to me and ask me what my secrets are. I just smile and then I tell Jamie that she should have kept her legs closed! Then all these people are taking my picture and asking me what I eat and how I stay in such great shape. Then this big producer comes up to me and says I am just the girl he has been searching for. He tells me how special I am and how he is gonna make all my dreams come true. And then I wake up and realize I am still in my boring existence in Nowhere Iowa. Oh well . . . What is a girl to do?

AMERICAN HWANGAP
Lloyd Suh

Dramatic
Esther, thirty-one

> *Esther is speaking to her father, who emigrated to the United States from Korea, left America to go back to Korea, and is back in the States again, hoping to reconcile with the family he left behind.*

ESTHER: You know the second man I married, Dad, he was just like you.

. . . We had a baby.

. . . We had a baby and I didn't want you to know, you didn't deserve it.

. . . I lost that baby, Dad, and I lost my fucking mind.

. . . That baby came out of me cold, do you get it? I lost him and I know that happens, couples lose babies and I know that, but things unraveled. That baby was gone and I'd already given him a name, we'd bought sheets, toys, books, and a car seat, Baby Bjorn and all that bullshit for the little guy, and he was gone like you were gone. And we were gonna try again, that's what you're supposed to do is try again, but I couldn't touch my stupid husband. I didn't want him near me, he smelled like you and he walked like you, this husband and surrogate you. I had to leave.

. . . I wasn't that unhappy when you left, Dad, truly. I wasn't unhappy until I realized what it meant that you left. Because I wanted a family so badly and couldn't get one. And you had it all the time, had it right there, and you didn't care.

. . . You gave me a purpose when you left, you stuck a void inside me, and I spent my life trying to fill it, but now that you're back, Dad, I feel so, so, so . . . well, I guess I feel free of it. Because you've come offering something I always wanted. But I know for certain that I don't want it anymore.

AMERICAN MAGIC
Gil Kofman

Dramatic
Woman, midtwenties to midthirties

The woman runs an interrogation unit. She is interrogating the Mind Reader, a man who is being held under suspicion of being a terrorist.

WOMAN: *(Enraptured.)* Oh my God! I can feel you thinking about me. How lightly you touch me with your thoughts. Like sunlight reaching across a million light-years of cold dark space to warm my cheek. Think of me. *Memorize* me. Make me yours. Oh God, I'm gonna come. Oh God! Oh God! Oh God! Look at me look at me look at me! *(She comes and quickly regains composure.)* What the fuck are you looking at?! You scum! *(Again, she closes eyes, begins to approach climax.)* Oh God this is incredible! You're doing it to me again. Oh God! No hands, no objects. Oh yes. My most intimate secret about to be exposed. What can be more *penetrating* than the transmission of pure thought. From my mind directly into yours. To be *mindfucked* like this . . . by a *mindfucker* like you . . . Oh God! *(She bites her lip as she comes. Then snaps to attention.)* Shhh! You hear something . . . ? I thought I heard something. *(Listening.)* Shh! Is it them? Are they back? Did you hear them? Better not to talk, not to think. *(Beat.)* Start thinking and right away you're in trouble. I swear, better to be an atheist than to question your own thought. Are you hot? Is it too bright in here? Thirsty? Are you hot? Did I just ask that? These are just some of the questions I ask myself every minute of the day.

AMERICAN SLIGO
Adam Rapp

Seriocomic
Lucy, thirty

> *Lucy is a single mom who works at the local Piggly Wiggly. She has been seeing a man named Victor, a shady character who has stolen her kid's Sony PlayStation console and sold it on the street.*

LUCY: Well, as you may or may not know, Victor and I have been seeing quite a lot of each other. We met while he was waiting in line where I work at the Piggly Wiggly on Pulaski Road. He was buying Bubble Yum and Poprocks. We went on a few dates: to the Olive Garden and to the old Dairy Queen on Caton Farm Road. Well, things moved a little quicker than I'm used to. You see, I was married in my early twenties and I have a son who is eight now — his name is Tyler — and after Tyler's father left, I felt very alone and afraid and I vowed I would never get involved with a man again. Tyler is in the third grade now, and being raised by a single parent has been hard on him, but since Victor's been around, he's had a male figure to look up to. They play catch and paint rocks and make copper etchings, and they've really gotten a lot out of each other, and I think Victor is adjusting quite well and, despite his problems with the law and his diabetes and substance abuse difficulties as well as the many emotional issues he's been dealing with, perhaps spurred by the death of his mother, in the few months since his release from the penitentiary in Marion, we've grown very close. But this morning my son woke me to tell me that he had just witnessed Victor leaving our apartment with his Sony PlayStation III console, which was Tyler's combination Christmas-birthday present. It's an item that took several paychecks to save up for it, and it's given both Tyler and I hours of fun and mother-son bonding experiences with games like Dark Cloud and Grand Theft Auto III.

So I came here not to punish Victor for slipping, as we all sometimes have to take a step or two back in order to move forward again, but to let him know that I support him and that if he returns the PlayStation III, not only will he be forgiven by Tyler and me and welcomed in our home again, but that he'll also grow from the experience. And just now while we were discussing this on the porch, he agreed to go find the large African-American man he sold it to on Wexler Boulevard and give him his money back in exchange for the game. What was his name again, Victor?

Big Nigga T, right. So after dinner, Victor's agreed to go find Big Nigga T and make things right.

ANIMALS OUT OF PAPER
Rajiv Joseph

Seriocomic
Ilana, thirties

> *Ilana is an origami artist, out on a date with a man she has just met,*
> *a high-school teacher who is a huge fan of her work. Here, she tells him*
> *why Valentine's Day brings back bad memories for her.*

ILANA: I just . . . I don't know, I've never been a huge fan of Valentine's Day.
. . . I mean . . . about ten years ago . . . My husband and I, we were
engaged at the time . . . I'm sorry. You probably don't want to hear this
. . . This is a . . . this is a pretty miserable story, but we were living in this
tiny old house. This wasn't *on* Valentine's Day, it was like a week before,
I think. And we both got really drunk and got into a huge argument.
And Demba . . . Demba was our dog . . . This was when he was only
about two years old . . . Demba would get really excitable, especially
when Mike and I would fight. So we stuck Demba in the garage that
night, because he kept barking and jumping around. You know, he was
a shepherd mix . . . a big dog . . . anyhow, we were drunk and we passed
out in separate rooms, and Mike passed out with a stupid cigarette in his
hand. And the house caught fire, and neither of us woke up.
. . . See, the house was a mess anyway . . . but I had so much paper.
Reams and reams of different paper, all over the place, hanging off the
kitchen table, the sofa, all over the place. It went up quick. But Demba
smelled the smoke, and he chewed his way through the door into the
house. The door was solid . . . a really strong, hard wood. And he broke
off most of his teeth, he got splinters in his gums . . . and he tore his way
into our burning house and woke me up and then woke Mike up. And
we got out. And the house burned down.
. . . So, Valentine's Day kind of always reminds me of being in the
vet's office, while Demba had splinters removed from his gums.
. . . Anyhow. Enough of that. Sorry. Not a great . . . I'm not the
greatest date in the world tonight.

BAGGAGE
Sam Bobrick

Comic
Phyllis, midthirties

Phyllis Novak, an unmarried woman in her midthirties, explains to Bradley Naughton, a disinterested divorced man in his late thirties, her reasons for still being single.

PHYLLIS: For your information, Bradley, all the breakups were my doing. . . . No, it's true. It's very true. I'm just too cautious. I want a hundred percent guarantee that my choice is going to be the right one, the perfect one. And as the relationship progresses, I always seem to find a flaw that starts out small, but one that I soon find so overwhelming I know I'll never be able to live with it. It could be anything, the way he eats, the sounds he makes when he sleeps, the TV shows he likes . . . I seem to be hung up on finding the perfect mate, which I know doesn't exist, yet I can't seem to make myself settle for anything less.

. . . Maybe that's the reason I'm being so open about my situation. I think I need to hear myself admit the fact that I have a problem. Since we don't really know one another and most likely won't see each other again, I'm probably more comfortable opening up to you than I would be to a closer and more sympathetic acquaintance. I know I definitely have a commitment problem and it's obviously bothering me. When I finally agree to "till death do us part," I want to be sure I have a shot at it.

BAGGAGE
Sam Bobrick

Comic
Phyllis, midthirties

> *Phyllis Novak has made up her mind to get married. Here she explains*
> *to the audience why she has remained single so far and how she plans*
> *to turn the latest Mr. Wrong in her life into Mr. Right.*

PHYLLIS: Let me explain how I've been thinking. Here I am, a very cautious, unattached, independent, not unattractive, woman, with no guy in sight and not getting any younger. OK, along comes Bradley Naughton, a guy who is not bad looking, clean, apparently no criminal record, has a good job, is emotionally needy and ripe for the picking with only one slight problem. He's not my type. So here's my plan. It's very simple. I will turn Bradley Naughton into my type. George Bernard Shaw sort of did that in *Pygmalion* and that worked out fine. It's not going to be that difficult. He's already beaten down so the resistance will be almost nil. I will simply win his confidence, make him very dependent on me, and what I don't like about him, I'll change. In no time at all, Bradley Naughton will be the perfect man for me. Trust me, when I finish with him you will like him so much more than you do now. And what about his hang-up with his ex-wife? Well, did you listen to him? In all the time he kept crying and moaning about missing her, did you once hear the word "love" mentioned? I didn't. That should tell you something. Anyway, I think it's a positive opportunity. Devious? Underhanded? Unethical? Yes. But in today's market, not a bad option for a single girl over thirty. Especially one as . . . spirited and picky and terrified about relationships as myself. OK, I know what you're thinking. What about love on my part? Well, I've been living without it so far, and as you can see, it hasn't affected me in the least. But it's time for me to settle down and I do believe Bradley and I can have a very nice life together. I promise you, it's going to work out fine. I'll have to write the airlines a thank-you note.

BEACHWOOD DRIVE
Steven Leigh Morris

Dramatic
Nadya, thirties

> *Having spent the night in jail after being arrested in a sting operation*
> *for prostitution, Nadya, a single mother from the Ukraine now living*
> *in Hollywood, is in the middle of an exit interview with a crusty LAPD*
> *vice detective in his sixties named Cromwell. The detective makes a*
> *number of offers to get information on the Russian mafia operatives*
> *who are running the prostitution racket; these include the dropping of*
> *all charges against Nadya and her transfer to another city where her*
> *aging parents, currently in the Ukraine, can join her under the um-*
> *brella of a witness protection program. "A clean start" is how Cromwell*
> *describes his offer. This is her response.*

NADYA: Fuck you. Fuck you and your new start. Give me one, give me one
good reason why I should trust you. Because you're the *police?* In this
city, there is not one, not *one* person who *ever* told me the truth, who
didn't *back* out of a commitment. I'm sorry, but that is my experience.
A lawyer I met. She wanted to be my friend. I said OK. I knit sweaters.
She wanted a sweater for her baby. Fine, I made her one. I didn't ask anything for it. But she said she would help me with my papers. I didn't ask.
She *offered*. When it's time to file my green card application, she's very
busy, getting ready to move back to Texas. OK, one rotten peach, you
say. But this happens time after time. You think I didn't try to open a
clean business here? You think I didn't try? Imported accessories from
the Ukraine. Handcrafted jewelry. Very simple, very classy, not folk, but
trendy, things that would sell here. I took them to a shopkeeper on
Franklin, we talked, we laughed, we told stories, I showed her samples.
She told me what was interesting to her, what was not. She placed an
order. I said, let's make a contract because the rings and brooches have
to be sent from Odessa. She says, oh it's such a small order, I'm good for
it, she says. I'm good for it. I spent money on that order, a few hundred
dollars, no, not thousands, a small order, but that's not the point. When
I call to make the delivery, my phone calls are not returned. When I

show up at the shop, she's too busy to see me. What can I do? Take her to court? This is the kind of truth I find in this city, time after time. Any idiot can make it through a crisis, it's the day-to-day living that kills you. That's from Chekhov. Vera, only Vera kept her word. Only Vera could get me out of trouble. Where I come from, when we break our word, we know the cost. The rules are clear. Our justice is clear. Your justice is a joke. Your jails may be filled, but what's that got to do with justice? Tell me why I spent a night in jail for an honest deal struck between two adults, while that shopkeeper, who broke her word, who cost me money, sits behind her booth, counting her money and making jokes about stupid Russians. And now I'm supposed to betray Vera for *you*. For your clean life? For your new start? *Fuck* you!

BRAINPEOPLE
José Rivera

Dramatic
Rosemary, thirties

> *Mayannah, a wealthy, possibly disturbed heiress of Puerto Rican de-*
> *scent, is hosting a dinner party at her mansion in Los Angeles. She has*
> *invited two total strangers: Ani, an Armenian woman, and Rosemary,*
> *who suffers from multiple personality disorder.*

ROSEMARY: Have I offended you? Whatever I said to you before, I'm sorry —
it wasn't *me* — *(Noticing the table.)* Oh my God, did I eat this shit? Excuse
me, but except for white meat, I'm a strict vegetarian!
 . . . *(Nearly gagging.)* This isn't funny. You just don't know what it's
like for me. I wake up with ticket stubs in my pocket to places I never
went to. On the street, women I don't know slap my face for sleeping
with guys I never met. I once woke up in jail — the things they do to
you in there, you'd never believe. At home I open my diary and the
words are in someone else's handwriting — the craziest shit you ever
heard.
 . . . Oh my God, how many of them did you meet? All of them are
imposters, no matter what they say. And each one, when they come out,
they think they're the center, the essence of me . . . but they're not . . .
there's only one, only me . . . I am Rosemary! *(From a pocket, she takes out*
a little wallet full of pictures, which she shows to Ani and Mayannah.) That's
me. The projects where I grew up. My best friend Tom before he died. My
mom's boyfriend . . . starting at thirteen, for years, he . . . look: a drawing
of me by Rosie. She draws me with horns and a tail because she hates me.
They all hate me. They've tried to kill me. They've put rat poison in my
food. You know how many times I've had my stomach pumped? They've
cut my wrists. And I'm just a real average girl who just wants a little normal happiness and no more drama and just maybe find someone to love
me and make a family with me someday . . . believe me —
(Like whiplash, Rosemary changes personalities, becoming Rosemary/
Rosario.)

ROSEMARY/ROSARIO: — when I say the one who says she's the real Rosemary is a liar. A killer. She's wanted for all those horrible murders in the projects. Mutilations. She's the one the police are looking for tonight. Don't trust her! HIDE THOSE KNIVES!

(Like whiplash again, Rosemary/Rosario changes personalities, becoming default Rosemary. She looks at the immobile, frightened Ani and Mayannah.)

ROSEMARY: — God, what are you looking at? What's wrong? What just happened? *(Beat.)* You don't believe me, do you? You think I'm one of them telling you stories. You don't believe I'm really here. *(As Rosetta.)* You're not here! *(As Rosie.)* You're not here! *(As Rosario.)* YOU WERE NEVER HERE!

THE CHOCOLATE AFFAIR
Stephanie Allison Walker

Comic
Beverly, thirty-three

*Beverly is speaking to the Halloween candy she has smuggled with her
into a cheap motel room to eat. Specifically, she's speaking to Mr. Good-
bar and M&M. They have just accused her of lying and stealing the
candy from her daughter, Sally, and are threatening to leave if she
doesn't come clean.*

BEVERLY: I'm up every day at five. Every day. Up at five, go for a jog, take a
shower, wake Sally, cook breakfast — something healthy — egg whites,
flax, kale, organic coffee, sprouted wheat. Sit down with Dave and Sally
for breakfast. Eat a tiny portion. Be sure to leave some on the plate. Always leave some on the plate.

Get dressed. Something feminine, flattering. Kiss Dave good-bye.
Make sure to give him a little something worth coming back home to.

Check on Sally. Comb her hair. Pack her lunch. Wait with her for
the bus. Hug her good-bye. Make sure that hug lasts all day long . . . that
she feels your arms around her even at recess when the mean kids pick
on her because their moms don't hug them enough. Then let go. Watch
her walk away, board the bus.

Choke back your tears. Taste the salt slide down the back of your
throat. Go back inside. Check yourself in the mirror. Ugh. Turn around.
Turn back hoping to see someone else. Cross through the kitchen. Pause.
Feel the quiet of the empty house. No one watching. What can you eat?
Open the pantry, look inside. Grab the jar of peanut butter. Unscrew the
lid. Take a whiff. Stick your finger in the jar of peanut butter. Lick it off.
Feel someone watching you. Shit. Turn around to face them. No one's
there. Put the peanut butter away. Wash your hands, careful to remove
any trace of peanut butter. Reapply lipstick. Head out the door. To work.
Again.

DEATH AT FILM FORUM
Eric Bland

Seriocomic
Hollis, twenties to thirties

> *Hollis is a contestant in an avant-garde filmmaking competition (a sort of*
> Project Runway*–type show to find the next American filmmaking au-*
> *teur). In the play, each contestant appears in a video monologue, explain-*
> *ing his or her point of view, dreams, motivations, and worries. This is*
> *Hollis's video monologue/interview. She speaks to the camera, similar to the*
> *way a person in a reality TV show might speak to the camera.*

HOLLIS: My life. It's really just a vast rush of synapse and hormones. Head and heart, you know? *(Beat.)* They come for me. Men. I'm not trying to get anyone's pity vote here. *(Beat.)* But I'm tired of going out to dinners where I'm expected to eat fondue. I don't want to anymore . . . because it's very boring, while you're letting your entrée sizzle in the oil, and you're wondering if you're doing it long enough not to get salmonella. I feel sorry for men because they go in the right direction but they cannot stop. Once you finally let them rub your back, very gently, over your shirt, which they do basically well, they're immediately trying to get under your shirt, to touch your back, your bare skin. They're like microwaves: if you don't put a timer on them, they just keep pouring more energy in.

I've been seeing some lately. Men. Am I mean to them? Men rarely describe me as mean. They're too busy trying, in very gentle and well-meaning ways, to suppress everything I have to say and flatter me into two-dimensionality. It's why I like being behind the camera. I'd rather flatten them out. Now I *have* heard women, oftentimes, refer to me as an incredible bitch. Which I like. I like it when others recognize you as competition. Otherwise, when you wallop them they get tears in their eyes and start to cry foul. Men. They're not as interesting as film. But there aren't as many people trying to do them, so if you want to get inside one — a man, not a film — and see it through to its conclusion, you can without selling your soul. If you're able to keep them at bay.

If you say things like, "I don't know whether I'm unhappy because I'm not free, or whether I'm not free because I'm unhappy." *Breathless.* That's from Jean-Luc Godard's *Breathless.* I'm saying it now . . . well, it's true. For me, right now.

DEATH AT FILM FORUM
Eric Bland

Seriocomic
Victhoria, twenties to thirties

> *Victhoria is the German curator of an avant-garde filmmaking compe-*
> *tition. She is hosting an end-of-competition party for the contestants. In*
> *this interior monologue, she speaks to her "friend," a person planted in*
> *the audience to whom she is able to express her inner thoughts.*
> *Throughout the play, Victhoria speaks with a German accent, but dur-*
> *ing this monologue, she drops the accent and speaks like a "normal*
> *American girl," a device that relates to both her state of mind and the*
> *monologue's content. At the end of her monologue, Scott, one of the con-*
> *testants (and the one whom Victhoria finds attractive), approaches her.*

VICTHORIA: Where's my friend? *(She sees him in the audience and waves him
up. He comes and she speaks with no accent.)* These guys, they are nice.
Nice people. I just don't know how to tell them the whole project has
been an incredible disappointment. Overall. Why can they not think
filmically? Why haven't there been any boats at sea, or bicycle chases, or
unbelievable monster costumes? Maybe that's what I implied I didn't
want. But it's a film, for Christ's sake. There's gotta be something to
watch. It's all become very . . . I don't know. Eccentric? Obsessive? On-
tological? Hysterical? I don't know about these guys. The girl, overall, is
interesting. To me. I understand her. I think like an American girl.
When I speak in my head, I speak like an American girl. I have to take
on shapes and maneuver quite cleverly to survive, like an American girl.
I understand her. Which makes me afraid of her. Maybe that's why I
eliminated her. Because, in a way, she reminds me of me. She would
vomit — but eventually she'll relent and become me. Moi. And you
might think, and you might think I'm about to poop on myself. But I'm
not. My life is pretty incredible. I live in theaters and galleries. I'm constantly eating in French restaurants. I have an affinity for German beer,
of course, and you don't know how many doors that will open up to you.
Try being a woman and sitting alone at a small table in any bar in the
city with a slender glass of German pilsner, knock it back in two gulps,
and watch the men crawl across the floor to press their dying bodies
against yours. As they try to make you smell the rot and bacteria buried

in their armpits or the odor coming from the tuck of flesh where the scrotum lies against the skin, or the matted scent, the smell like a door-mat, that comes off their chests where their wiry hairs thatch to retain all the oozings and olfactions of their various pores and glands. I can't stand a man's perfume, a stupid whiff of cologne — they are so bad at masking themselves. Why pretend tonight? For Calvin Klein or Giorgio Armani? Why shout flowers or citrus in a high-pitched squeal when, once you nestle in beside me or I remove your undershorts or sniff the scruff on the back of your neck, I hear nothing but the undeflectable low-wave frequency that is the bellow and roar of your stink, of your hormonal, fetid stench, of your every desire, you who right now desire little more than a gleeful-as-a-schoolboy-in-a-bathtub-with-a-photo-of-a-plump-naked-woman-touching-her-giant-areoles bout of sex. *(She sees Scott. Back to her German accent.)* Want a whiskey?

EQUIVOCATION
Bill Cain

Seriocomic
Judith, nineteen

Shakespeare's daughter muses on her fate. Her father lavishes endless attention on fictional characters and barely notices his living, breathing flesh-and-blood child. Though Judith's father is more famous than most, her situation as a daughter is — unhappily — not that rare. Her grace, intelligence, and humor will see her through.

(Judith surveys the audience, then speaks to them.)
JUDITH: I don't like theater . . . And I don't like soliloquies. *(Judith crosses out a soliloquy. Then.)* So it's odd that I'm the one who has them.

(To audience with disgust.) Soliloquies. People you've never met telling you things you'd rather not know . . . Because nobody ever tells anybody anything *good* in a soliloquy, do they? It's always somebody who just killed his father telling you he's on his way to sleep with his mother. If anybody did that in real life . . .

(Rewriting.) But people do it in plays as if it was the most natural . . . Because — in plays — everybody's got a secret story.

(Nonsense.) And he always gives them to the wrong people. As if you needed to know one more thing about Hamlet . . . He should give them to minor characters — people's daughters, for instance.

(Then.) But that wouldn't work, would it? According to him, a daughter's job is to love and be silent. So — there'd be nothing to say . . . Besides, who would listen?

ESSENTIAL SELF-DEFENSE
Adam Rapp

Seriocomic
Sadie, twenties to thirties

Sadie is talking to Yul, a very strange, possibly demented man whom she met at a self-defense class where he works as a padded dummy, sort of a human punching bag. Sadie has fears that threaten to overpower her and sees in Yul something of a protector.

SADIE: So I want to tell you something, Yul, and I don't know why I'm telling you because I hardly know you and I haven't shared this with anyone — not even Sorrel Haze, and she's my best friend. By the way, is that OK — that I just used your name in the middle of a sentence?

. . . Good. I'm glad . . . *(She gathers her will.)* You see, Yul, I've been having this problem lately where I think something horrible is going to happen to me. It's a little hard to explain, but I feel terrified almost every minute of every day. In bed at night. At the office. While selecting fruit in the produce section at the grocery store.

I live on the top of Hill Street. In a little blue house with white shutters. It's a pretty modest house, but it has a yard and an excellent view of Norvis Woods, and lately I've had this insistent feeling that a beast — a sort of yellow-eyed half-man half-wolf — is going to come creeping out of the woods intending to harm me. I see him walking upright. With mangy fur and preternaturally human hands instead of paws. For some reason, I can't get him out of my head. Just last night I couldn't fall asleep because every time I closed my eyes I saw him standing over my bed with those hands. His yellow eyes glowing. It was so real I could almost smell his breath.

And it's not only the wolf man; it's other things as well. For instance, last week I was buying stamps at the post office and I almost became paralyzed with the fear that I was going to be abducted. By who, I don't know. The security guard had to escort me out to my car.

And I don't really know where this comes from, because nothing's really ever happened to me. I've never had an experience like you with those kung fu rollerbladers. I've never been harmed. I'm not a rape survivor. I've never been afraid of the dark. I haven't received any threatening phone calls. I'm generally not even intimidated by the idea of a horror movie. It's just this unmanageable crushing feeling of terror and helplessness.

FAULT LINES
Stephen Belber

Dramatic
Jess, thirties

> *Jess's husband, Bill, has accused his best friend of moral culpability in the death by suicide of a young female college student with whom he had a one-night stand. Her husband also thinks something may be going on between his friend and his wife. Here, Jess lays into her husband.*

JESS: No, Bill. But the day I *do* will be the day *you* start shoving your warped vision of "morality" around in *other* people's faces.

(She turns back toward the door, but then turns back again.)

And if you can't handle the fact that if we hadn't met, that Jim and I, in some parallel universe, might *be* together, then you are living in a hole in the ground! If your perspective of our relationship is confined to seeing me as a stay-at-home baby machine in your little warped vision of domestic bliss, then our marriage is a crock of *shit*. People *have* a capacity for attraction beyond the person they live with, Bill, even sometimes for the best friend, and for you to be thrown into a *morally judgmental tailspin* upon the realization of that — at *this* stage and at this *age* is *unbelievably* pathetic! *(Now quietly intense.)* If this is the way you treat someone after nineteen years then I fucking *shudder* to think how you might treat *me*. Or your child. *(Quieter.)* For that matter.

50 WORDS
Michael Weller

Dramatic
Jan, mid- to late thirties

Jan's husband, Adam, has just confessed to having an affair. Jan is bored with their marriage and is unable to give or receive love or even affection. Here, she tells Adam why this is.

JAN: No, Adam, I'm normal. I'm what normal people are like. You think my mom sounds crazy, you should meet some of her St. Augustine club ladies. "Pillows of the Community," they call themselves. Charming wives and mothers, but just under the surface they're all looney-tunes, most of them driven to it by pretending for years and years to be happy wives and mothers, but they'd never up and ruin everyone's life by blabbing the truth, they don't call little Jimmy into the kitchen and say "You're a spoiled, ungrateful drain on this family, and dealing with your incessant demands has caused me and my husband to fall out of love with each other, so why don't you take this one-way ticket to Bhutan and stay there until you're financially independent and able to do your own laundry," and they don't tell their poor hubbies "Honey, you were always kind of boring and predictable, but you're becoming a sort of parody of yourself lately, plus you're putting on weight, which is very unappealing, and I hate that aftershave you use, not to mention the things I learn about your digestive system when I do the wash." No, we don't say these things, we drink some wine and we smile, and we expect our husbands to act with the same restraint and refrain from telling us when you're fucking other women, we do not want to know that — Too Much Information, Do Not Share, thank you.

FROM UP HERE
Liz Flahive

Dramatic
Grace, forty

> *Grace is sitting in a police station. Her second husband, Daniel, age thirty-two, has just arrived after hearing from the neighbors that she was brought there.*

GRACE: I didn't intend to assault anyone. I was trying to help. While you were on your "break," I was trying to help everyone. I walked into the kitchen, and Kenny's in there with Kate, his mentor, practicing his speech. And he's standing up completely straight. Looking out. Do you know how long it's been since I've seen him stand like that? It was going so well. But she's like all the other people keeping him at a distance. And I wanted to kill her. I was so angry I probably could have . . . And I tried to touch him, and really, he barely looks at me. He'll look at Caroline. He'll look at Lauren. He'll look right at you. But he won't look at me. And then they left for the dance, and I was sitting in the kitchen alone and I . . . I couldn't be in that house anymore, I couldn't be in there, so I walked outside to get some air and calm down. And those gardeners were finishing replanting next door after that pipe burst, and they were packing up. So I walked over to check in with Bonnie, see if everything was all right, and I see this man, one of the gardeners, on our lawn. He was hiding in the bushes on the side of the house. And his pants were down. And he was going to the bathroom. On my lawn. On our lawn. He's outside, exposed, on my lawn, quietly shitting on my lawn, like it wasn't anything, like this was something he did all the time, like crouching behind a hydrangea bush made him invisible. And I ran over there screaming, I was screaming, and you know I can really scream, you've never actually heard me scream. It's so loud. Shocked the hell out of me. And I ran up to him and I kicked him. Hard. Right in the ankle. All the time screaming and screaming . . . I guess all the other women in the neighborhood turn a blind eye because his face . . . He looked so surprised. And I started hitting him with my hands, and I grabbed his shirt and pushed him down and put his face right near his mess, and I said, you're going to clean that up, you don't shit on people's lawns. Who do you think you are? I live here. My family lives here. And he started crying, saying something I couldn't understand, full of shame and anger. And then I started crying, apologizing to him over and over, so now we're both there. Sobbing. And that was when I went back inside, and I started throwing everything away. I'd see something and I'd pick it up, take it outside, and drop it at the curb. Plates, furniture, pictures, all your clothes. And then I knocked down the mailbox. And that was really satisfying so I knocked down the Kirschenbaum's mailbox across the street. Then . . . well, then the police came over. And brought me here. That's what happened to me. How was your day? What happened to you?

GEE'S BEND
Elyzabeth Gregory Wilder

Dramatic
Sadie, early forties

> *After defying her husband, Macon, to march across the Edmund Pettis Bridge in Selma, Alabama, Sadie returns home to find that he has locked her out of their house.*

SADIE: Macon? Macon, where you at? Open the door. *(She pounds on the door.)*

My eyes. I can't hardly see. They put gas in our eyes. It burns real bad like. I need you to help me. It was real bad there. Bad like you never seen. They beat us, Macon. They was waiting, and when we come up over that bridge they took after us. I put my eyes straight in front of me. Walk strong, I be thinking. Walk strong. I so busy looking ahead, I don't see what come up from behind. Sky goes black and me, I'm on the ground. Taste the blood. But I know the hurt mean I'm still alive. They beat on us, then left us for dead. Folks in they stores all up along the way, they just stand there and watch. We cry out, but don't nobody do nothing to help. Please, Macon. I know you say don't go. But I had to. That man he be beating on me, and I say, Sadie, you stand up. I ask the Lord to give me strength. That man might beat me down, but the Lord he raise me up.

GEE'S BEND
Elyzabeth Gregory Wilder

Dramatic
Nella, eighty-one

Nella, now old and senile, stands at the water's edge waiting for the ferry to take her to town. She is telling her sister, Sadie, about watching their possessions being taken when she was a child.

NELLA: They didn't give us no warning. Nothing. Mr. Rentz, over in Camden, was the man doing the furnishing for us. But then Mr. Rentz dies and his widow decides she want it all back. I come running down the road. *Mama, they coming. They got wagons. They taking everything.* Mama standing there on the porch, big ol' butcher knife in her hand. She send the little ones in the house. She say, *Nella, take this knife. Want you to go out to the barn and kill them two hogs. The babies too. Take the knife and slit they throats. They ain't taking my pigs.* I love them baby pigs. *You big now. Go on.* All the way down the road, people standing on their porches and watching as the men ride through. Wasn't long before a man come with his wagon. Don't even speak. Just starts taking. Took Mama's milk cow that was out in the yard, shovels and buckets. He just about to leave when he hear them pigs back in the barn. They screaming something terrible. He looks to Mama, standing there stone-faced, and he smiles. He take off toward the barn. But then the screaming stops. And here I come, covered in them pigs' blood. He got one look at me and he take on off outa there. 'Bout that time Daddy come running in from the field. But it was too late. He chase after that man until he fell down in the dirt. The only time I ever seen my daddy cry. That man was broke down. Mama roast them pigs, but I couldn't eat. Can't hardly stand the smell of pork. I do what Mama say. But it ain't right.

GOOD BOYS AND TRUE
Roberto Aguirre-Sacasa

Dramatic
Elizabeth, late thirties to early forties

> *Elizabeth's son Brandon, an A student and star athlete at an exclusive*
> *Catholic prep school, has made a video of himself brutally forcing a girl*
> *to have sex. He has denied it's him on the tape; but his mother knows*
> *he's lying.*

ELIZABETH: You think so? You think he'll understand that three weeks ago, his
son — his son who has *everything*, his son who is in the enviable position of being able to afford *whatever* future he wants for himself — that
his son drove to a mall specifically looking for some poor girl to, to *ex-
ploit?* What were you *thinking*, Brandon, while you were getting ready?
Were you thinking: "I have to find a girl who's not that pretty, but pretty
enough. Who will do certain things, things I'd *never* ask Erica to do. And
not only must I do these things with her, I have to *prove* that I did them,
so I either have to *convince* her — No, that's not right, there's no *way*
you could have convinced the girl to let herself be — be *used* like that.
Not even as charming as you are — as *handsome* as you are. Brandon, do
you want me to get the tape back from Russ so we can watch it together?
(Silence from Brandon. She continues.) Because this is what *I* saw, when *I*
watched it . . . I saw a boy — *I saw you* — lead that girl onto, what? Not
even a bed, onto a *mattress*, on some floor . . . I saw her *smiling* at you
because she didn't know what you were about to do . . . (How *could* she?)
I saw you turn her around — flip her onto her stomach — and ease her
up onto her hands and knees . . . I saw you grab her hair — and pull on
it — and push into her harder and harder . . . I saw you slap her. I saw
you force her face into the mattress, so — why, so you wouldn't have to
hear her? (What was she saying . . . ?) I saw you — I couldn't see your
face — but I swear, you were *enjoying* it, Brandon.

GOOD BOYS AND TRUE
Roberto Aguirre-Sacasa

Dramatic
Elizabeth, late thirties to early forties

> *Elizabeth's son Brandon, an A atudent and star athlete at an exclusive Catholic prep school, has made a video of himself brutally forcing a girl to have sex. Here, she confesses to him that his father was involved in something similar when he was a young man and that she was complicit.*

ELIZABETH: I went to see Russell . . . Then I went to Montgomery Mall . . . then to Garrison . . . and walked around there for . . . hours, looking at the girls, trying to remember what it was like . . . What I was like . . . I talked to the girl; I talked to Cheryl. She's tough, isn't she? *(Quick beat.)* And smart, too. I *liked* that; I hope it means she's going to survive this. She reminded me of a girl from Garrison, whose name was . . . This is Ancient History now, but it was Alice, Alice Kinney . . . *(She looks at him.)* Alice transferred in our junior year, she wasn't someone we'd grown up with, which made it more difficult for her to, to acclimate. And she so desperately wanted to be in, to be one of us . . . And the way she decided she was going to do that was to land a boy, the *right* kind of boyfriend. From St. Joseph's, or Gonzaga, or Landon, or — really, it had to be one of those three. *(Beat.)* Our junior year, there was a party, at a boy's house, from St. Joseph's — *(Asking him.)* — and the host of this party *was* . . . ? Your father, yes. Who asked me to invite Alice, which I thought was incredibly . . . *generous* of him . . . And I planned to keep track of her, throughout the night, but Alice seemed to be doing fine, and I was . . . with your dad. So I, more or less, forgot about her . . . Until around midnight, when your dad and I were in a gazebo, in front of his house, talking — (and we *were* just talking) — and one of his friends came up to us and said, "It's happening, right now, hurry!" And your dad, he leapt up and ran off with this boy — and this other boy was . . . Russell. Around the house, to the back of the house — I followed them — and they were all there . . . Your father, Russ, their teammates . . . And one of them was up on a ladder that had been set against the house, and he was . . . peering into a window, up on the second floor. Your father and his friends had organized a windowsill party . . . Those don't exist anymore, do they? Inside that room, Brandon? On the second floor? Alice Kinney was losing her virginity to a boy from St. Joe's, and the boy's friends — your father included — were taking turns, watching them . . . I stood there; I saw them climb up and down that ladder, one by one . . . *(Beat.)* And it had been *planned* . . . And I had *participated* . . . I knew . . . I knew something . . . *(Beat.)* I had an idea, when your dad asked me to invite Alice, of what was coming . . . And part of me, when I *really* look back on it, when I *really* force myself to, Brandon . . . part of me *consented* to it happening . . . *(Almost rationalizing.)* If it happened to Alice, and if she became dirty, or damaged, or spoiled — and she did, she left midterm, we were cruel to her after that night — but if our boyfriends did what they wanted to Alice, then maybe they wouldn't do it us . . . That's what they did, what they were going to do, to someone, and . . . better her than us. I'm ready now, I think, for all of it, everything. I'm ready for you to say it. *(Beat.)* Do you realize — and *accept* — and *own* — that you did something horrible — *beyond* horrible — to Cheryl Moody? The way your father and his friends did — and I did — to Alice Kinney?

HENRY AND ELLEN
Don Nigro

Seriocomic
Ellen, forties

Henry Irving and Ellen Terry have been acting together for many years and are the greatest acting pair of the late Victorian period at Henry's theater, the Lyceum, in London. They have been lovers for years and continue to work together. Although they have married other people, they still love each other deeply. A catastrophe has just occurred: a fire at the warehouse storage facility has destroyed nearly all the costumes and sets that Henry has been accumulating for thirty or forty years. Ellen has found Henry alone on the stage of the empty theater and has come to console him. Alone in the empty theater, both are filled with memories of the great work they've done together, their love for each other, and a sense of the eerie holiness of the place.

ELLEN: I remember as quite a small child being brought backstage late one night by my parents. Somebody'd forgotten something in the dressing room, I think, and I got bored and wandered out onto an empty stage in a dark theater like this one and stood staring out into the darkness, and I felt like I had stepped into the very center of the universe, into the very middle of the labyrinth of God's brain, and you could look out into the great dark and see the galaxies turning so lovely and sad and cold, and the hackles at the back of my neck — what are hackles, anyway? One among the multitude of things I don't understand and never will, but of course you know, don't tell me, you always know everything. What an infuriating man you really are, Henry. But in any case, I would get these goosebumps all over, the chill of the empty spaces would just overwhelm me, this sense of mystery and completeness, and of, for once in my life, not really wanting to be someplace else, doing something else. I was where I belonged, as it were. Of course, then one grows used to things and gets bored with all the rubbish one must wade through and some of the really dreadful people one must deal with, present company excepted, and I gradually forgot all about that feeling. It grew very, very ordinary for me by the time I was eighteen, and it stayed ordinary then for a very long time, until I met you, Henry. For, in spite of the fact that you are occasionally unendurable and drive me right to the edge of insanity, you know, Henry — you know, I just forgot what I was going to say. That's another one of my great gifts, a terrible memory, which is, however, contrary to what one might think, actually a great advantage to an actress, because it enables one to promptly forget one's disasters, which of course I must have had in great abundance, if I could remember any of them, both artistic and private, though mostly private, I think, but in any case, Henry, why do you talk so much?

HILLARY AGONISTES
Nick Salamone

Comic
Hillary, sixties

Hillary Clinton has just been elected president. Sixty-five million peo-
ple — one percent of the world's population — have disappeared, First
Husband Bill Clinton among them. Madame President has just made
a reference to "the rapture" in a public address — a televised prayer cir-
cle in the Rose Garden — saying, "The seeming rapture is upon us."
Following this prayer circle, Treasury Secretary Michael Bloomberg cor-
ners Madame President in the Oval Office, incensed that she has made
such an overt religious reference, fearing that any hint that the world
may be ending will destabilize the planet's financial markets. Madame
President, in this speech, explains the political reasons for what she said.

HILLARY: Well, they're not very goddamn good fundamentalists are they,
Mike, if they're still here?
. . . If it were the literal rapture — not just the seeming one — then
why are they still here? And Bill and Jane Fonda and fucking Kim Jong-
il gone! Kim Jong-il, Mike! For godsake!!! What kind of God snatches
up to his bosom the Stalinist dictator of North Korea?! What kind of
rapture is that?! Of course the fundamentalists don't really care about
North Korea. They're still obsessed with Bill. That's the beauty part!
That's why the Republicans are acting so crazy! It's not because they're
ashamed that Jesus left them behind. It's *Bill!* How do they explain Bill!
I swear to God if Bill hadn't disappeared I would have had the CIA kid-
nap him and hole him up somewhere just so I could say he had. Don't
you see, Mike? Bill's our ace in the hole. No one's going to believe this
is the real rapture — least of all the fundamentalists — if Bill is among
the rapt.

A HOUSE WITH NO WALLS

Thomas Gibbons

Dramatic
Cadence, thirties

> *Cadence Lane, a controversial, conservative African-American author, tells a white friend, Allen Rosen, about the tumultuous reception she received at a lecture appearance on a college campus.*

> *(Cadence, in comfortable but stylish clothes, standing with a glass of wine in her hand.)*

CADENCE: The first time it happened, just after "The Race Circus" came out — five months ago? — I was so surprised. Bewildered, really. That male voice hurtling out of the darkness with such anger. I thought some guy was having an argument with his girlfriend. The rest of the audience was shocked, it was obvious. But it came again, aimed at me from another part of the auditorium, a different voice but the same rage — unreason — in it. I just had time to think: I've been set up, this is an ambush. Then it erupted from a dozen carefully chosen spots in the audience.
  (Softly.) "No More Lies. No More Lies."
  (Pause.) They wouldn't stop, they wouldn't listen. Suddenly every-one was shouting — at me, at each other . . . "Stop the lies!" "Let her speak!" Things, small dark objects, were flying through the air onto the stage. I actually was afraid then and started to walk off, my foot crushed one . . . and I saw what they were: Oreos. Now it's a regular attraction of my appearances. A conservative group on some campus books me to speak, knowing it will outrage the liberal groups. Particularly the black ones. And they snap at the bait — they want to be outraged, outrage is their manna. I begin to speak, after a few minutes someone interrupts, the cookies fly, and we all enter the funhouse of self-righteous campus politics. The cons accuse the libs of stifling free speech. The libs accuse the cons of fascism and racism. Everyone postures and shouts until the security guards move in. Then they all go back to their dorms to — *(She shrugs.)* — get drunk and fuck, I suppose.

HUMAN ERROR
Keith Reddin

Dramatic
Miranda, early forties

> *Miranda is a single woman in her early forties. A crash-site investigator for the National Transportation Safety Board, she has recently returned to work after a nervous breakdown. On her first assignment, she begins a tentative affair with a coworker, Erik. Here, she relates the end of her previous relationship and the effect it had on her.*

MIRANDA: The last time I saw David, he was forty-five minutes late. We hadn't talked in months, I was a wreck, as I've said. But he was coming into town, and he called me and said, let's get together, I need to talk to you about something important. And I said, can we talk about it over the phone, and he said, no I need to see you in person, and I begin to think he wants us to try again. Try and see if we can make this thing that was us, if we can salvage it. And the next morning he calls twice to change the time we're going to get together, and this pisses me off a little, but we finally settle on this time, and like I said, he's really late. I was about to go and I look up and he's standing there in front of me. He looks tired and old. Older than I've seen him. I knew he had been traveling, but still he suddenly looked so . . . He had gained weight and he was losing his hair. He seemed so . . . vulnerable. And I was feeling all the old emotions, sure that we could get back to where we were. And he sits down and right away orders a drink and then another, and I'm wondering when can we talk about things. But he's going on and on about these deals he's involved in. How he's so close to making all this money. And then he finally takes my hand, and he looks me in the eye, and he asks me for money. He asks for quite a lot of money because he has this deal lined up and it's a sure thing, and I realize that's the reason he's here. It's not about the love we have for each other, or how he's sorry about the hell he put me through, or the lies he told, or the other women he slept with, or the drugs he took, he's here to get money. Something clicks and I know we can never go back to what it was we had. And I tell him I can't do that. Give him the money, and he tells me how disappointed he is. How I'm being shortsighted and letting my emotions ruin a perfectly good opportunity to increase my investment, and pretty soon he tells me he's got a plane to catch and how great I look and we'll talk soon. And leaves. And I end up paying for his drinks. And I go home and I don't go out for a week. I just lay there on the couch and I don't go out and I don't answer the phone and I don't show up for work and when I finally do surface, my boss tells me I need counseling, and I feel like everything I gave, my entire being I gave as a gift to this man, all of my love, my very soul, that part of my life, it's the past, not the present. I loved him, but there was no way we could ever be together. And the realization just hammered me. But I knew I had that love in me. And it's only now that I'm beginning to . . . I'm here. Just here. And it's one thing I can talk to Ron. But it's another that I tell you all that.

So. Let's get back to work.

THE ICE-BREAKER
David Rambo

Dramatic
Sonia, late twenties

> *Sonia Milan is a Ph.D candidate in climate science, as impulsive as she*
> *is brilliant — a dangerous combination for a scientist, exacerbated by*
> *her need for attention. Now, having been derided by her peers but dri-*
> *ven by a passion for her ideas, she's tracked down a reclusive mentor*
> *whom she hopes will validate her work.*

SONIA: Frankly, Dr. Blanchard, my conclusions are scary . . . I need to know
if my assumptions are correct, if I've asked the right questions, before I
take this any further.
    . . . Sure you can. *(Beat.)* My thesis — my whole career in science
— started with that journal. I wasn't even interested in geology until I
read it, and then — wow! — ice ages every hundred thousand years.
Who knew? I loved the idea of recapturing ancient oxygen. Listening to
what it has to tell us. And where we really need the ice to talk to us —
the ice at bedrock, the ice from the last time the planet was at the end
of an interglacial — there's silence. Or, at best, confusion. I'm like you
— couldn't resist that mystery. That's why I went to college, and now
grad school, and to Greenland, and back to Antarctica, and to a drilling
platform over the Sargasso Sea picking over putrid sediment cores — to
be the one who hears what the bedrock ice is telling us . . . *(Beat.)* Or
trying to, anyway. So we can figure out what happens next. I know I'm
onto something. And it's important. And if what I need can't be found
at the bottom of the ice cap, then tell me where else you think I should
look. *(Beat.)* I can't get anyone of any stature in the field — especially
Bob Chernoff — to help me. *(Beat.)* Either this breaks new ground, or
it's the pathetic scribblings of a lunatic.

IRENA'S VOW
Dan Gordon

Dramatic
Irena, twenty

> *Irena Gut, a twenty-year-old Polish Catholic woman, is speaking to the*
> *twelve Jews whom she is hiding in the basement of a German major*
> *without his knowledge. She works for the major as his housekeeper and*
> *has managed for almost a year to keep the Jews hidden in the basement.*
> *Now, however, one of the married women, Ida Haller, has announced*
> *that she has become pregnant. Her husband, Lazar, as a kind of*
> *spokesman for the group, has asked Irena to procure what she will need*
> *to perform an abortion because a baby would jeopardize the safety of*
> *the group. This is Irena's response.*

IRENA: Is that what you think, Ida? There's no choice? Do you want to have
a baby?

... This isn't just a matter of religion. I saw a baby ... ripped out
of its mother's arms and killed in front of me while I stood by and did
nothing ... could do nothing ... I saw that baby's mother shot to death
in front of me and I could do nothing. And I made a vow then and there
to God that if I ever got the chance to save a life I would and that's why
without even thinking, I took you here to hide you. Because of that vow
... But I was wrong ...

(She looks at Ida.) And you taught me that ... It isn't enough just to
save a life ... to preserve a heartbeat ... to simply survive ... We have
to live ... We have to live in the face of death, otherwise, the Hitlers and
the Rokitas of the world have won and have turned us into, what did
you call it, Lazar?

(She crosses to Lazar and searches his eyes.) ... rats in the darkness?
Isn't that what you said? That we couldn't just be rats living in the darkness?

(She turns back to Ida.) Ida ... if there was no Hitler ... no Rokita,
no ghettos, no camps, no S.S., no Major Rugemer upstairs, would you
keep this baby?

KINDNESS
Adam Rapp

Dramatic
Frances, mid- to late twenties

Frances, a sexy and mysterious woman, has wandered into a hotel room shared by a teen named Dennis and his mom, who has gone off to a Broadway show (Dennis didn't want to go). Who is she, and what does she want? Here, Frances tells Dennis what has been going on. The problem is, is any of this true?

FRANCES: Look, Dennis, this is what's going on: For the past ten months I've been seeing a man. A very wealthy, very powerful, very charming, very well known *married* man who owns a Fortune 500 company and who is old enough to be my father. About three months after we started seeing each other, I got pregnant from this man. And shortly thereafter, he asked me to get an abortion. I wanted to keep the baby. He didn't. He already had four children — all adults now — and he wanted no part of that. He offered me a lot of money. And ultimately, a deal was struck to the tune of a hundred thousand dollars. Money I was to be paid immediately following the procedure. We went to a very exclusive, private clinic. Things were really hard for me after that. And when I say hard, I mean hard to be alive. Hard to see his face. Hard to be reminded of the loss. Hard to not feel like I was floating around in someone else's life. But somehow the most difficult thing of all was the realization that the money was never going to come.

Since I've been feeling better, we've been meeting here in the city, where he rents me an apartment and pays me a generous allowance. But to keep things neat, we rarely stay there. In fact, we mostly tuck ourselves away in places like this and he pays cash and uses an alias, covers all his tracks. But the more we met the more the subject of the money seemed to fade.

So, this weekend I made a special arrangement of my own because, you see, one can only feel like a fool for so long. And about twenty minutes ago, after he unwittingly swallowed a powerful sleeping pill and passed out, he was photographed by a major tabloid photographer, for which I was handsomely paid. So he's currently lying facedown in his birthday suit in a room on the floor below this one, almost directly under the ice machine. And soon I will take the elevator down to the lobby, get in a taxi, scoot across town to Grand Central station, and board the last Metro North train up to Rowayton, Connecticut, where I will take yet another taxi to his ridiculously large house, where his wife is no doubt sitting in front of their stainless steel, monolithic espresso machine, throwing back vodka tonics and wondering where her husband goes every Saturday night. And I'm going to knock on their door, and when she sees my pleading face, she's going to invite me in, and I'm going to sit down with her at their kitchen table and direct her to a website where photos of yours truly and her husband pleasuring themselves in several highly compromising positions are on display. And then I will show her a set of Polaroids just to drive it home. And then I'll tell her how her husband and I met. How and when we fucked for the first time. Our rendezvous at the various midlevel hotels around the city. The vacation to London where he told me he loved me on Waterloo Bridge. The black-market Viagra dealers we've gotten to know. How he needed me to bury my finger halfway up his ass so he could come. The night we spent in Mount Sinai's emergency room because he thought he was having a heart attack. The dresses he bought me. The pearls and the earrings and the three-thousand-dollar shoes from Bergdorf's. The restaurants and his fucking cronies who would all but grope my ass when he was in the bathroom pissing out multiple martinis. All the trimmings, of course.

And then I'll tell her about the pregnancy. And the abortion. How it all went down. The private clinic and how gently he held me in the back of the limo on the way home.

And I'll tell her about the hundred-thousand-dollar promise not kept. And about the strange faith that he had that our affair would survive all of this.

You see, Dennis, he had a chance. I decided that tonight was his final opportunity to make good on the money. But before he got in the shower, just a few minutes after we fucked for our final time, I asked him about it, and he said that it wasn't going to happen. He called me stupid and told me I was lucky to still be in his life.

So earlier when you dialed that number and hit pound you set it all in motion, Dennis. You cued the photographer to make his way up from the lobby. And after you fell asleep, I went downstairs and met him and undressed and crawled under my ex-lover's body and made erotic fuck-me faces and went down on his flaccid penis and positioned his face just right for the camera. Hell, I even strapped one on and got a little kinky. And a few minutes ago, I went back there and gathered my things and said good-bye to his body. Which looks somehow smaller while he sleeps. Feeble even.

LOVE LOVES A PORNOGRAPHER
Jeff Goode

Comic
Emily, twenties

> *Emily, the daughter of Lord and Lady Loveworthy, has just returned from the American Wild West with her American frontiersman fiancée, whose name is Earl. (Her parents misunderstood her letter telling them she was coming and thought she was marrying an earl. Imagine their surprise!) Loveworthy is a novelist. His guests for tea, when Emily arrives, are his neighbors, Rev. and Mrs. Monger. Monger is a literary critic who detests Loveworthy's books. He and Loveworthy have been arguing the whole time, and Emily has had enough. Plus, somebody has to do something about the body in the backyard.*

EMILY: You are all such horrible, beastly people! I thought, coming here today, having returned from America with a string of fresh vices, a poor choice of husband, and an ill-considered tattoo, that I, for once, would be the talk of the tea and not this perpetual peevishness. But I see now that one may travel the world in search of depravity and never find so much of it as lies heaped in one's own backyard. Or in the garden. You are all abhorrently boorish and whorish and rude, and were I not related to some of you, I should love nothing more than to have nothing more to do with you for so long as I live. But as we are not entirely unrelated: Father, I shall expect you at my impending wedding, to give me away with your blessing. And Mother to weep. And thereafter I shall endeavor never to speak to either of you ever again. Mr. Monger, it has been a pleasure to meet you and your lovely wife, and a horrible embarrassment. And my condolences. Earl, come with me. We are going to move a body. Again!

LOVE SONG
John Kolvenbach

Dramatic
Joan, thirties

> *Joan is a hard-driving no-nonsense professional type with little or no*
> *patience for incompetence. Here, she is telling her brother Beane about*
> *an epiphany she has just had.*

JOAN: I wrote his book reports.

   . . . Because I loved him more than life itself.

   . . . Then he left me for that new girl with the jeans.

   . . . That night, I was up in my room. (You remember this?) It was dinnertime and Mom kept calling —

   (Yeah, God, "hoo-hoo"), and I was sitting on the edge of the bed, and I was Crying. *(Beat.)* Just heaving, you know, the end of the world, Snot. You know that thing, you're crying so hard you can't make space between the sobs to Breathe. *(Beat.)* I was touching myself. For comfort, I dunno, I had my hands down my pants. *(Beat.)* He had that yellow bicycle.

   . . . And so there I am keening and masturbating, I'm sloshing around in six kinds of fluid . . . and I can remember Seeing myself. Observing myself from above, looking down at this *puddle. (Beat.)* I remember thinking, very distinctly I remember thinking: Look at that. Look at her. How I've been Rendered by this boy. This shallow boy, this Paper Bag has Obliterated me, *look* at that. *(Beat.)* And I said, "This is the last time," out loud, I actually swore to myself, The Last Time that I will be made a *Fool* of by Feelings. *(Beat.)* I zipped up my pants and wiped my face on the sheets and I started my life. *(Pause.)* I jumped my husband yesterday. *(Pause.)* I kissed his feet and made him scream like a baboon and I cried on his shoulder and lay there next to him and traced pictures on his stomach with my finger.

MANNA
Cheri Magid

Dramatic
Bess, twenty-six

Bess confronts her sister about the lies she's been telling her for the past three years.

BESS: I can't believe you. I can't believe you would go to such great Herculean efforts to just totally royally fuck with — do you know why I came here? Do you, Maddie? I bought you that fucking poncho. The one you were looking at at Bloomingdale's last week when you thought I was still paying for your fucking day planner. And I knew you would never buy something like that for yourself even if it would look great on you, and God knows you need a new jacket. So I went back the next day on my lunch hour, and I bought it. And I wrapped it in this pretty paper and I overnighted it and I couldn't fucking wait. I couldn't wait for you to show up for coffee or or to the gym wearing this cute little knit little springy thing, but then I go back, I go back to the office the next day, and what is on my desk? Your package. Your fucking package with this great "delivery refused" sticker stuck across the front of it. So I called you, but the phone — nothing, nothing fucking happened, so then I tried you on the cell phone that I gave you, but all I could get was my fucking voice on the fucking voice-mail message. So I went to your building, the one I've driven you "home" to three, four, seven different times since I've moved here, and I buzzed 3F and I buzzed 3F and something in my little pea brain must have snapped because all of a sudden I was just buzzing all of them all at once until finally the super comes out and tells me, yeah, he knows you, sure. But you haven't lived there in three years. Three years? Three fucking years! And then I'm like oh my God, OH MY GOD. "Oh no Bess, you can just drop me here, I need to go to the Korean deli." "Oh no Bess, this is fine, I need to mail a letter." "Oh no Bess, you don't want to come up — the downstairs neighbors are doing all these renovations, your allergies will go fucking ballistic."

MANNA
Cheri Magid

Dramatic
Madeleine, thirty-four

Madeleine speaks to the audience as she builds her dream bakery.

MADELEINE: Let us make unto ourselves a space: thirty cubits and a half shall be the length thereof, and twenty cubits and a half the breadth thereof. And westward shall be two large windows — a fine sunny exposure, a sweet savor unto the Lord. And the location therein shall be at 119 Avenue B, even at Seventh Street. And it shall be unto the people a shrine of gastronomy, a beacon of Alphabet City. Let in this space there be an outer room; fifteen cubits shall be the length thereof and twenty and one-half cubits shall be the breadth thereof. And upon the hinder part of the outer room shall be a display case of glass and of silver, wherewith to show our cakes. And affronting the case shall be four tables, each of acacia wood — two cubits by two cubits — and may the tables be adorned with cloths of the finest gingham and dried flowers and let the flowers hang even from the ceiling. And moreover upon the walls, let there be vintage signs and folksy wonders, a fine Vermont in the midst of the city. Let there be a curtain dividing the outer room from the inner, the holy from the holy, the work of the weaver in colors. And the cloth shall be like that of the curtains of the windows, of fine twined rayon of blue and white checker work. And let the hinder part be lined in plastic so as to be germ resistant. And let this curtain be forever drawn so that all behind it be as sacred and as wonders. Behind the curtain eastward, let there be an inner room. And let there in this room be the instruments of the kitchen in all the service thereof. A bread kneader and a bread couche, a sheeter and a proofbox, stone-hearthed ovens, and even shall they be self-cleaning. And round about this room let there be chrome racks where shall be kept the dishes thereof, and the pans thereof, and the jars thereof, and the knives thereof, and the bowls thereof, and let them be of the finest materials, of cast iron and aluminum, of Calphenon and Le Creuset, of Fagor and of Cuisinart. In the hinder part of the inner room eastward, let there be an office separating the holy from that which is most holy. And into this place shall only the chef go. None shall enter who hath not been purified. And it shall be a sweet savor unto the Lord, a memorial before him continually. Finally, let us fashion for ourselves holy garments, for splendor and to keep clean. Let us clothe ourselves in a tunic of loose-knit cotton blend and breeches of checker work. And round about let us envelop ourselves in an apron of fine-twined linen, of scarlet threads, and let this apron be embroidered with our name, Miriam's, above the heart. Let us for our feet choose sneakers of fine white canvas with ergonomically correct insoles and air cushions for comfort. And we shall adorn ourselves with a spoon of silver and a rolling pin of gold. This is a holy place, blessed be it!

THE MULBERRY TREE VARIATIONS

Don Nigro

Comic
Madchen, early twenties

> *Madchen is a young girl whose whole life has been spent on a remote*
> *South Sea island, where her widowed father is the jailer. She's speaking*
> *to Jack, a troubled young sailor who's been thrown in jail for acciden-*
> *tally killing another sailor in a bar fight defending her honor. She*
> *brings Jack his meals and is falling in love with him. She has spent most*
> *of her childhood sitting under a mulberry tree reading. She is desperate*
> *to get off the island and out into the world so she can have adventures.*
> *She's just realized that Jack is from England and has seen London, and*
> *she's very excited by this information. She's a girl with a vivid inner life*
> *and a tremendous amount of energy who's had nobody to talk to in a*
> *very long time.*

MADCHEN: Never put mulberries in your pocket. That's what my grandfather
taught me. He was my mother's father, and when the mist would creep
in off the ocean, he'd get his shovel and bury large objects in the garden.
Once he buried the cuckoo clock because it wouldn't shut up and drove
the cat mad. And one night when the mist cleared, he showed me the
planet Venus. All I could see was a bright splotch of light by the moon,
but Grandfather said, look closer. Look with the inside of your eyes and
you can see a naked woman. Of course, Grandfather saw naked women
in his chowder. He was an old sea captain who'd been whacked on the
head by a flying yardarm, or a flying Dutchman, or a flying squirrel —
something flying. He brought that mulberry tree from China, along
with a helmet made of an old wasp's nest and a deck of round cards with
windmills and labyrinths on them. When Mother married Father,
Grandpa never spoke to her again. But when I was very small, my
mother's ghost would lure me over the broken wall to play in her father's
garden, and despite his worst intentions, he came in time to love me. Intense passion runs in our family. That's why most of us are dead. For

three nights in a row he dreamed of a burning mulberry tree. I found him in the garden being picked apart by crows. They'd taken his eyes. Well, just one eye, to be fair to the crows, since the other eye was glass. So I was forced to transfer my affections to his mulberry tree. We pass love from one object to another in a doomed attempt to revisit a place we've never been. And yet there is much to be said for mulberry trees. The purple juice from the fruit makes mulberry wine, and the silkworm eats the leaves and spins her cocoon, and when she wakes, she's somebody else entirely. What are you looking at? You'll make me nervous, and I'll never shut up. I swear to you on my mother's grave I can go for months hardly saying two words, but I babble when I'm nervous, and you make me very nervous because you seem so familiar, as if I'm remembering you from a time that hasn't happened yet. Or perhaps I've dreamed about you. Dreams are the closest thing to truth we have, next to sexual intercourse and stories. I used to dream about a hideous creature shuffling down a cobbled London street to kill me. It seemed more real than life. But I recommend great caution about trusting dreams or love, because dreams can kill, especially dreams of flaming mulberry trees, and the only thing that buys love forever is the losing of it. If you're going to kiss me, now would be an excellent time.

THE ONES THAT FLUTTER
Sylvia Reed

Dramatic
Woman, thirties to forties

The woman is speaking to Roddy Haynes, the central character in the play, who is a warden at a maximum security prison. She represents a property developer who wants Roddy to sell his family home and land to the developer.

WOMAN: Do you know how many people would kill to be in your position, Mr. Haynes? It's like winning the lottery. My mother plays every week. The same numbers. She says it's gotten to the point where she can't not play. Because she's afraid that'll be the week those numbers are called. But here you sit holding a winning lottery ticket and the only decision you have to make is whether or not to cash it in. *(Stares hard at him.)* I've picked a bad time to drop in, haven't I? I can tell. I tried to call ahead and this time I didn't even get your answering machine. I don't know if you're aware, but your phone doesn't work. I couldn't get through. Is this a bad time? *(Silence.)* All right, then. I don't know what your story is, but . . .

(Looking around the living room.) The Milligans' walls were filled with family pictures and Mrs. Milligan showed me every last one of them. She took me through the history of her family, and you want to know what was hard? Sitting down and trying to go through these plans with a family like that, with a history like that, trying to show them what we had in mind for the land they love. And they were more than gracious. She baked lemon squares! She set them out on a pretty china plate and offered me one. *(Silence.)* Mr. Haynes? . . . Mr. Haynes? Are you all right? Mr. Haynes? You'll be the only one left out here.

(Looks for response, waits, doesn't get it.) I hope you realize that. I'll leave these plans and the paperwork explaining our offer for you to look over when you're feeling better. But don't take too long. The deal does have an expiration date.

(As she exits.) I'll be in touch.

A PERFECT COUPLE
Brooke Berman

Dramatic
Amy, forty

Amy is speaking to Emma. The two have been best friends since college.
Amy is about to be married. Emma is defiantly single.

AMY: You used to want to get married. You can't wait for things to happen, Em. Use your will. Make it happen. Take action. Every single step of the way, I'm the one who has made MY relationship "happen." And it's all working out. We are finally getting married. We have dated, we have taken breaks, we have broken up, we have seen other people, we have gotten back together, we have been long distance, short distance, we live together, we bought a condo, sold it, made a profit. We went through an abortion, a new business, two of his fellowships, weddings of all of our friends (except for you). — And who is the one who constantly makes it OK to take each new step? Me. I am the one who does this. I do this because I can do this. Because I am not afraid. Because I had good parenting. I am the one who knows it is permissible — no, pleasurable — to take Next Steps. So. I am the one who laid the ultimatum on the table, and Isaac responds really well to that. I give him structure. He needs that. He loves me for the structure I impose. Because otherwise, he'd be lost. You may think you know Isaac, but I can attest to the fact that without me, Isaac would be lost — stranded — literally — in an airport somewhere, between flights, on a layover, lost. We meet each others' needs. Find a partner so that you are not alone. Get practical. Realistic. Change the kind of men you date. Change your expectations. Change your whole way of doing things. In fact, I've heard, I've heard people say, if you just start doing every single thing in a new way, you will get new results. Look. I love you. I love you, and I want you to be happy like me.

PERFECT HARMONY
Andrew Grosso and The Essentials

Comic
Melody, seventeen

> *Melody McDaniels is the first three-year pitch and president of the
> Ladies in Red, her high school's female counterpart to the world-famous
> The Acafellas, the boys' a cappella group, who are seventeen-time na-
> tional champions. The Ladies in Red have never won a national com-
> petition, but Melody is convinced that this might be their year — if
> only she can imbue the other girls with her own confidence. (Note:
> During her speech to the other girls in the Ladies in Red, Melody's
> supreme confidence extends to her vocabulary, and she is unaware of
> her malapropisms.)*

MELODY: *(Looking at her cards, back to the speech. She's practiced this before.)*
Ladies in Red, I'd like to hand a rose to each of you as a thank you. A
thank you for having ideas and trying your best. But best is, of course,
relative. We've been to nationals the last two years, and we've never come
away with the prize. We've each tried our best, but The Acafellas have
won each time. Why do the boys win? Because they have confidence.
They have confidence that the group sounds good, so they do sound
good. It's a self-refilling prophecy. After yesterday's rehearsal, it's clear we
still don't have that confidence. So last night I went home and defecated
on the situation and I produced a solution. This year, I'm not just giving you a rose, I'm giving you my confidence. Mickey, I give you my
confidence that you can learn to sing a song using only the words from
that song. Valerie, you will learn to be looked at while you're singing —
I'll give you that confidence. And this CD reminding you that I'm looking at you — you can play it and practice being looked at. And finally,
Meghan. Meghan Beans, I know we haven't always seen with the same
eye-to-eye, but underneath that mess of unnecessary movements, you
have a lot of natural undisciplined talent. And enthused asthma. And I
see that. And you have a point about the solos. And I see that too. Yes,
I'm the first three-year pitch and president in Lady in Red history, and

I've been recognized for my arrangements twice at nationals, and I won Best Female Soloist last year, but we still came in seventh. A chain is only as strong as its weakest link — we saw that with Valerie's unfortunate panic attack. And we're seeing it this year with our background. So, I will sing backup. Meghan Beans, ever since 1988, "Wind Beneath Our Wings," our signature song, has been a very special song to all of us in the Ladies in Red. It's usually given based on proven competence not just shrewd presidential hunches, but this year we're polishing every link. Meghan, I hand you my trust and our signature solo. *(She "knights" Meghan with the rose wand.)* Snaps to you, Lady in Red.

PERFECT HARMONY
Andrew Grosso and The Essentials

Comic
Mickey D, fifteen

> *Micheala "Mickey D" Dhiardeaubovic is in her second year in the*
> *Ladies in Red, the girls' a cappella singing group at her high school.*
> *Throughout the play, characters address the audience directly, as if*
> *speaking to a schoolwide assembly about the "a cappella crisis."*

MICKEY D: *(Relentlessly cheerful.)* Hey. Hello. Hiiii. My name is Micheala
Dhiardeaubovic but I like to be called Mickey D, and I'm in the Ladies
in Red. It was just lucky that I in group. There was a girl in Ladies in
Red would been, what you say, knocked in? Knocked on? Knocked up?
Knocked up. So they emergency put me in. And I love the singing in
English. The words sound so nice. I used to sang in my brother band in
Herzegovinia before the accident, when my parents get, how you say,
eaten by tractor? So we come to America. And I love you it. Ladies in
Red are like community. I can do the talk, you know, talk to other people, not just my brother. The friends are not like your family, not like
your stupid brother who only talk about the Sex Pistols and trying to
play war doctor with you. And we do the dance is so fun you know
dance. I love you all the girls. They my the friends with me. Everybody
want to do the beat the boys to the win, but they get a little so uptight,
you know, crazy about the this or the that, sometimes they have like a
fruit up their butt that needs to be juiced. Melody needs to be juiced
with the fruitness. They have to loosen up and let it all hang, hang, hang
down. It's not healthy to always, the words so specific. I just sing, sing,
sing with your soul, with your heart, and let the juice flow out, the
words are not so, you know, let it out.

PERFECT HARMONY
Andrew Grosso and The Essentials

Comic
Kiki Tune, thirties to forties

Kiki considers herself a "talent packager." She's a poor man's Svengali who
has made it "big" with a few boy bands and girl bands. She's interested
in potentially signing one of the high-school singers in The Acafellas or the
Ladies in Red, two high-school a cappella singing groups. Throughout the
play, characters address the audience directly, as if speaking to a school-
wide assembly about the "a cappella crisis." Kiki has some definite opin-
ions on that and, in fact, on just about every issue.

KIKI TUNE: Can I smoke in here? Nazis. Look, education comes in all shapes and
sizes. I'm an educator. If I sign one of these boys, I can educate them on the
world. I got three touring groups right now — one in Vegas, one in Dussel-
dorf, and one in Scranton. That's education. The truth is sex sells. Do you
think people like listening to a bunch of boys turn a sexy Prince song into a
eunuch's tone poem? NO. But they love those young faces. They love watching those underage Adam's apples bobbing up and down. They love seeing
those hard bodies spank that song like the bad girl that needs to be disci-
plined. But there is competition. Sex is everywhere you look now. So you
have to sell the good sex, not the I'd-rather-be-watching-PAX-TV sex. You
you think Kiki Tune's wrong? You know my track record in this business. I
found Syncopating Spunk in Orlando and turned them into one of the
hottest acts of the country. Not this country, but let me tell you something,
Moldova is a hotbed of a cappella superstars. Don't let anyone tell you any
different. Five number-one singles they had. Kiki doesn't go platinum by
being wrong. Have you seen my house? It's a great house. It's the only pink
stucco two-story ranch in Florida. Here in the U.S. of A., a cappella is a firm,
pink, untapped market. But you gotta tap it the right way. You can't just stick
the tap in anywhere. Look, it kills me to break the Acaboys up, but I only
need one. It's sad they give up their eligibility to sing with their cute high-
school groups, but if you want fame, if you want platinum, if you want
stucco, you gotta make choices. You want education, that's education.

RABBIT
Nina Raine

Dramatic
Bella, thirties

> *Bella is meeting some friends for drinks. They are a very contentious lot*
> *who include her ex-boyfriend, Richard. Here, she responds to his charge*
> *that she has become angry and hard-hearted. It is what she needs to be*
> *to stay sane.*

BELLA: Do you know *why* my father always thinks he's right? And that I'm
wrong?

. . . No. Because I'm a woman and he's a man. Deep down, pri-
vately, he doesn't think women are as good as men. Nearly as good, but
not quite. That's why he reminds me of you. So my mother will *never* be
as important as him . . . And my father thinks — he loves me very
much, he loves us all very much — but deep down he thinks — my
brothers are the talented ones. The clever ones. They're the ones he's
proud of. Not me.

. . . And it makes me feel competitive. Angry and competitive. I
think, you're wrong. I'll be tougher, and harder, and better. Because I'm
right. Women can be better. *(To Richard.)* I did see it from your perspective, Richard. I felt what you felt. Jealousy. But I think it comes with
love. And I decided not to be in love. I didn't want to feel it. I decided
to be hard. Like you said. And I know I ruined it. And I'm sorry. *(Beat.)*
I felt it with you. *(Beat.)* And it felt — it didn't feel like I thought it
would. Because it felt — more than anything else, in the end it felt —
competitive and angry. I thought, you're not going to treat me like shit.
I'm going to treat you like shit. First. I ruined it when I tried not to care.
And I ruined it when I did. *(Beat.)*

. . . Competitive.

. . . And I lost. *(To Richard.)* And you think that makes me into a
person who doesn't believe in love. You think I've decided to be a selfish,
domineering, hard person. And I think you're a selfish, domineering,
sentimental person. I annoy you. And you annoy me. But you're right.

I am deliberately hard, domineering, and selfish. And you know why? Because I saw my mother wasting her whole life on other people. Mainly my father. And I don't want to do that. *(Beat.)* And last night I couldn't get to sleep until three in the morning because my head was full of the people I've neglected. *(Beat.)*

. . . And it isn't going to be worth it. It isn't worth trying to be a success. Because it's not going to work. *(Beat.)* Why did my dad try and teach me Latin? *(Beat.)* See, I don't always think I'm right. That's where you're wrong, Richard: wrong, wrong, wrong.

. . . Where are the great women? Last night I realized — all my favorite authors are men. Why aren't any of my favorite authors women? *(Beat.)* And it's not just writers. Composers. Conductors. Artists. I just don't think they're as good as the men. I don't think women are as good as men.

. . . So there you are, Richard.

RUNES
Don Nigro

Dramatic
Evangeline, thirty-six

> *Evangeline Wolf was impregnated as a girl in the backroom of her fa-*
> *ther's general store one December night by a person she's always insisted*
> *was a Bible salesman named Jack Pentecost, now deceased. Soon after,*
> *she married Arthur Wolf, who has loved her since childhood. Never*
> *happy in her marriage, and tormented by the sound of the little bell*
> *above the door that rings whenever anybody enters because it reminds*
> *her of the night she was attacked, she has finally abandoned her fam-*
> *ily. Arthur was found shot dead in the store one night, and their daugh-*
> *ter, Vonnie, a brilliant but enigmatic girl who's obsessed with casting*
> *runes to tell the future, is about to be charged with his murder. Here,*
> *Evangeline tries to make sense of her life.*

EVANGELINE: I close my eyes and they come to me in fragments. Memory and
regret. Like the stones Vonnie threw on the table. You try to see how
they connect. I loved my children, but sometimes they were like chains
around my neck, pulling me down into the water, and I had to get away.
I'd go downstairs in the dark at night. I have bad dreams. A dark man
walked by the window and looked in. There was such sadness in his eyes.
Jack Pentecost, I thought. He's come for me at last. I ran out to look,
and the bell rang above the door, but he was already walking over the
bridge. I cried out for him to wait, but he kept walking, disappearing
into the falling snow. I ran after him, but I kept losing sight of him in
the darkness. And when I was so exhausted I could barely stand, and my
bare feet were torn and bloody and nearly frozen, some people in a
wagon picked me up along the road, and I went with them. But I kept
thinking about my children. And I couldn't bear the thought of having
left them with you. With a monster like you. A monster who loved me.
Who had the gall to love me. After what I did. After who I was. After
what happened in that little room, when the bell rang above the door,
and he came to me with so much need and so much sorrow. To love me

after that. How could you love me after that? To love me after that is unforgivable. So I made my way back home, and I found the shotgun there on the counter, like a sign from God. And there he was, asleep at the table, waiting for me, as I knew he would be. And he opened his eyes and saw me, and he smiled. There were tears running down his face, he was so happy to see me. Then I raised the gun and pulled the trigger.

THE SEX HABITS OF AMERICAN WOMEN

Julie Marie Myatt

Dramatic
Daisy, twenties

Daisy is explaining to her concerned parents why she doesn't want to get married.

DAISY: The old maid won't embarrass you anymore tonight. She's going home to her cats, her books, and her rotting bed.

. . . I saw you whispering. I saw you. Clicking your tongue in disappointment and shrugging your shoulders, Mother. I saw you. I heard you. "Fritz and I just don't know how she got this way. And she won't let us help her." "We've tried everything." "We don't know what she does, but she sure scares those men off." — "By the way, do you know any single men? But, God knows, give her Prince Charming, and she'll probably throw him away too." . . . "Give her a frog to kiss and damned if nothing happens."

. . . Stop! I don't want to be married! So stop! Just stop! You stop embarrassing me, Mother, and I'll stop embarrassing you. OK? Let's make a deal. We'll just call it a truce. You take the chip off your shoulder, and I'll stop crying on it. OK? You too, Daddy. You don't have to carry it. You're done. I'm alone and staying that way. You can rest in peace. You don't have to take care of me. It's not your fault. I'm alone. Live with it. Done.

SNOW
Adam Szymkowicz

Dramatic
Sara, twenties to forties

> *Sara is speaking to Ed about her concerns and their present and possibly future relationship. In the context of the play, this monologue occurs during a brief flashback scene in which Ed describes his failed relationship with Sara.*

SARA: There are many things I do not understand, although I am an intelligent person. There are things beyond my grasp — things that screech or howl out numbers. There are darknesses I cannot comprehend. There is death somewhere and somewhere black holes and tears in our unconscious. Somehow the brain works, but how I couldn't tell you. One day my heart will stop and so will yours, but at this moment, we sit beside each other with our beating hearts and our pleasant faces. We are afraid, you and I. We are terrified people. Many people aren't as terrified as we are. They slip through life without concerns or wants. They don't worry about what they know but instead they purchase things and eat up every new TV program. These people are happy, and perhaps we should be more like them. But we are not, and no one can control the weather. Try as we might, we are only these creatures with two legs, maybe a soul, some of us a God, all of us hearts beating until they don't. And I will stay here with you because it is what I want. I think it is what you want too. And we will work towards some design perhaps or maybe just screw, but either way I will be happy for more than a few moments and maybe someday when we are old, we will sit holding hands looking out the window at the snow falling.

SPEECH AND DEBATE
Stephen Karam

Comic
Diwata, teens

Diwata is a theater geek who has started her own podcast. This is her first entry.

DIWATA: Welcome to the first podcast entry of my diary, updated daily at monoblog.com. Let's hear it for my band — that's Casio in the background. Casio's been programmed to play the only three chords I know over and over while I improvise a new song, live, before your ears, America. Ideally, the music would be a little more interesting, but I can't play and sing at the same time, and I have no friends to help me out. "But Diwata," you're saying to yourselves, "you're so odd and frumpy — you must have friends." But no, I don't. All I have is my music. There is music in my body. Nice. The upcoming auditions for this year's spring musical were the inspiration for this *live,* streaming musical entry. My high school will be doing the timeless classic *Once Upon a Mattress,* and this year, like every other year, I will not get cast because of my talentless drama teacher — a man I'll call gay-guy-with-a-receding-hairline in order to protect Mr. Walter M. Healy's anonymity. But this year, I think *America* should decide whether or not I get to showcase my skills in North Salem High's multipurpose room. "But Diwata," you're asking, "how can we show you our undying love?" Calm yourselves, I'll tell you. You see, Mr. Healy was foolish enough to include his e-mail address on the bottom of his class syllabus; so I say, let the e-campaign begin: If you think that I should play the lead in the spring play, write to the fool at dramedy at aol.com. That's D-R-A-M-E-D-Y at aol.com. Mr. Healy, this verse . . . is for you. *(Singing.)*
    Mr. Healy, you're a crap sandwich
    I'm pure and you're a crap sandwich
    Get some bread, your balding head, and some more bread
    You have your head between bread
    Crap sandwich . . . yeah . . .
Fierce. I totally improv'd that.

STRETCH
Susan Bernfield

Dramatic
Rose. seventies

> *Rose is Rosemary Woods, formerly President Nixon's personal secretary.*
> *She is in a nursing home, and her mind comes and goes. Here, she has*
> *gone back in her mind to the time of Watergate and is trying to persuade*
> *her boss not to let a trivial thing like Watergate destroy his presidency.*

(Rose stands in her spotlight.)

ROSE: Mr. President, the wolves are at the door.
Mr. President, I'm not sure I can keep them out anymore.
But I can keep it up, keep circling the wagons.
And I can keep a straight face.
And I can keep things running, keep a secret,
keep whatever, whatever you need me to
you know I can as well as you know
anything.

I have tried with my body and my brain
I have typed and stenoed and delegated
I have stretched
for Judge John Sirica and all the media
liberal and less so
I have shown them my moves
how I reached for the phone
and my fingers slipped onto the wrong button
recording over your conversation, four, five minutes at most
a *terrible mistake* I said in court, yet a simple one
I have stretched
and I have heard the snickers from around the world
because I know that you — you!
I have seen you do the utmost good
I have seen good
good.

Twenty-three years of service, of respect.
Eighteen and a half minutes of buzz.
Hum. Absence of conversation.
And nobody looks at me anymore
without asking a question.
Erasure.
For all my efforts, I have made the cover
of *Time* magazine
it was always a dream of mine — Secretary of the Year!
You and I know that secret is not always bad.
Inner circle, they spout that like an indictment
but is anything more indicative of mutual trust?
Is anyone more without reproach
than the mutually trustworthy?
When you're in the position you're in
Mr. President
who should you want around you?
Strangers?
There are some protections
the Secret Service doesn't offer.

Mr. President, I have done my job.
You have dug yourself out of the doghouse before.
But this time it's wolves at the door.
They are nipping at our ankles
your ankles, you!
Who have done so much for our nation!

Done so much good for all of us!
I am telling everyone!
The president will never resign!

And Jeane Dixon says,
Jeane Dixon says that everything will turn out fine.
May will be a bad month, May and June, probably
but everything will turn out fine.
And isn't she the greatest psychic our
nation's ever seen? Isn't she the one who predicted
that God would make you great?

It makes me think — one of the first things I learned
when I moved to Washington.
When I transferred to your office, Mr. President,
when I became secretary to a senator.

The floors are slippery in the
corridors of power.
Cold marble, cold and slick.
Don't wear your best heels.

THE SUNKEN LIVING ROOM
David Caudle

Seriocomic
Tammy, late teens

> *Tammy, described by one character as an "Ambassador from Slutland,"*
> *is talking to her boyfriend Chip's younger brother Wade about her*
> *lifestyle, a preliminary to trying to seduce him.*

TAMMY: I'm a freak. Because I smoke pot and have sex and skip school. There's one freak in student government, but she's really a brain, who's just a drug addict with mental problems. Mostly freaks don't go in for student government. I think some of the *brains* have sex, too, and drink a little beer sometimes, but they're in a *lot* of clubs and student government. The rednecks drink beer and have sex and skip school, but some of *them* are in student government. The *jocks* drink beer, smoke pot and have sex and skip school, but still some of *them* are in student government. *(Beat.)* That's what Chip is. A freak-jock. If he didn't have black friends he'd be a freak-jock-redneck, 'cuz he's also friends with some of *them,* and I know he's bagged a few of the *brain* chicks, so actually you could say he's a freak-jock-redneck-brain, pretty much just across-the-board kinda guy. *(Beat.)* Except he's not in student government. *(Beat.)* Me, I'm just a freak. And you're just a brain, right?

. . . I mean, you don't smoke or drink or skip school or . . . any of that, do you? . . . Don't you ever wanna know what it feels like?

. . . I guess that's good in a way, but aren't you supposed to be, like, trying things out and *testing boundaries?* That's what the guidance counselor says I'm doing . . . She says it'll be good for me in the long run. But she said I shouldn't tell anyone that she said that.

. . . Don't tell anybody I told you that. I don't want to get her in trouble. She's really cool. I think she smokes weed, actually. Once I thought she was about to offer me some, but the vice principal came in. I actually think she digs me. You know, like lezzz be friends. It's cool, though.

THERE OR HERE
Jennifer Maisel

Dramatic
Robyn, late twenties to early thirties

> *Robyn, a breast cancer survivor, spends her nights talking on the phone with Angelina, an outsourced tech-support operator in a call center in India. The two have forged an intimate relationship that spans the thousands of miles between them, even though they have never met.*

ROBYN: I'm not asking you to solve it for me. People think that's what I want to hear, but it's not. Ajay thinks that, but I just want it to be done. You know — they say remission, they won't say cured. They say there's a five-year waiting period. And then they say be vigilant and then they say don't stress. I will admit to having a calendar tucked in the back of my desk, and every day I cross out another box, but the months, the years I have to go — I can't help it, they loom. I know you told me to meditate, and I did, I meditated. I went to a class, even. Ha. So I decided for the three years and seven months left of the "wait and see" to like my rage, to embrace my rage. Love it, cuddle it, nurture it, and fuck it. Why not?

They tell me to expect the unexpected, but that is impossible. They tell me to let go of expectation and *that* is impossible. We're not hardwired like that. People here or anyone anywhere. To be without expectation is to be without anticipation and the potential of joy — I mean, what do you like better: the hand moving towards the crotch or the hand on the crotch? For me, hand toward because once it gets there, it's probably not going to do exactly what you want anyway. And I think — the rage, maybe the rage isn't a problem. I mean, the rage has been with me in some shape or form my whole life, and I can't imagine why the rage would want to make me sick because then the rage wouldn't have a home at all. The rage is my child. The rage is all I've got these days to keep going.

THREE CHANGES
Nicky Silver

Dramatic
Laurel, late thirties

Laurel's husband, Nate, has just lost his job and is slowly losing his mind. Laurel has begun to realize the meaninglessness of her own life.

(A light comes up on Laurel in the living room. She's carrying a plastic tray divided into many sections. Each section is filled with buttons. One section holds pearl buttons, another toggle buttons, another bamboo buttons, and so on. She addresses the audience.)

LAUREL: It's a box of buttons. I spill them on to the bed, then I mix them up with my hand and Nate sorts them. And then I mix them up again, and he sorts them again. And so on and so on. And so on. You see, Nate wasn't "fine," despite his protests. He was in pieces. For a couple of weeks after that, two weeks, he went through the motions. He printed out résumés and sent them to people that he thought would care. They didn't. The answers came back as silence . . . And I just don't think he has the courage, or the energy, or the vision, to begin again. So now he spends his days in his pajamas. He doesn't talk much. He doesn't watch TV; there isn't much to watch. Sometimes when I'm at work, he plays cards with Hal, who really has been a blessing. But Hal needs time, he has to work. And so in the evening, when I come home, I spill out the buttons. I learned this trick from my mother. When I was a kid, twelve, I guess, or thirteen. I was sick. I had a penicillin reaction— I'm allergic to penicillin — and I spent the summer in bed, between baths of calamine lotion. Twelve years old, all day in bed. I sorted a lot of buttons. That was the summer Diana got married, Princess Diana. I remember watching it and crying. Everything looked so beautiful. I didn't dream of being a princess, I didn't have the nerve. My dreams were small, really, suburban . . . Just a child. Someone I could take care of, who would love me . . . I named him Adam, and he was perfect. When you lose a child, still inside of you, people don't know what to say. They don't know where to look. It wasn't, after all, a person. Not yet. It was just an idea. It was just a promise. But it's gone. It's dead. And there's nothing anyone can say. No one wants to dwell, that would make it real. You don't have a funeral. There's no place you go to say good-bye. People say "I'm so sorry" and then they change the subject . . .

(Near tears.) I knew the children that lived inside of me. I understood them. And I loved them . . . and they loved me. We decided, Nate and I, after the third time, that we should stop. So we did. We didn't try anymore. That's when I got depressed, after the third time. Nate thought, he assumed, it was for the baby, that I was mourning the baby. But I wasn't, not really. I don't think that's why I got depressed. I think it was because, and this is just embarrassing, and I know it isn't very modern, but I think it was because, you see, it occurred to me, in the absence of children . . . I didn't know why I was here. I mean, I work. I have a job. I shop. I cook. I talk to people on the telephone. . . . But I couldn't figure out why. All of a sudden the big questions presented themselves and I didn't have the answers. I functioned. I got dressed. I did my job. I tried my best to just fill each day, even as it stretched in front of me, like a thousand years . . . But I didn't know why. To lay out a catalogue that no one cares about? To pretend that I'm happy for someone else's benefit? . . . I couldn't find an answer.

(She looks away briefly, embarrassed by her terrible sadness.) The funny thing is, I never did. I just learned how to stop asking the question.

(She composes herself.) I should take this into Nate. He'll be awake now and feeling bored and lonely.

(She exits. Black out.)

THE TUTOR
Allan Havis

Dramatic.
Mrs. Bentley, early forties

*Mrs. Bentley addresses her son Orson's tutor, Seth Kane, insinuating
that her husband assumes she is having an affair with him.*

MRS. BENTLEY: I think Orson's very attracted to you.

. . . You probably conform to some fantasy figure in a graphic novel.
I love the word — graphic. Do you? You make him laugh, Mr. Kane. He
believes you have a natural irreverence.

. . . We all need a good laugh.

. . . You amuse me in a quiet way and for that I find you endearing.
And I stopped noticing men years ago.

. . . George must have filled you in. It was quite a scandal.

. . . Orson was lucky. He nearly killed a homeless man at a city in-
tersection . . . Orson is wired differently from other boys. Maybe he's just
like his father. Neither George or Orson have any sense of remorse about
their actions. They only believe in luck. You would think they have
stones in their heart. They must be reptilian. And as a result they don't
feel deep hurts of others. But they damn know the distinction between
right and wrong. They know how to argue for the underdog. And they
always win. If they are wrong, they make it right. Because words are full
of tricks. I don't expect you to instruct Orson on ethics and moral be-
havior, because you might as well teach a monkey to sing. Well, actually
I saw a monkey sing on Animal Planet cable and I was very impressed.
Is this all crazy talk? I must be very lonely, Mr. Kane. And that's worse
than ovarian cancer. *(Back at the window.)* Maybe the city police are
working for George. George's always buying cops drinks and dinners at
this tawdry strip club downtown. What's it called — "Sugar Tits Sally"?
He's too cheap to hire a private detective, even if it's tax deductible. And
when George's drunk, he's unbearably jealous. Or course, George thinks
I'm sleeping with you at Motel 6. High-style adultery. And what the hell
can I say about that?

UNDER THE POMEGRANATE TREES

Don Nigro

Dramatic
Patty, nineteen

> *In the backyard of an apartment near the campus of Arizona State*
> *University in Tempe, in the autumn of 1968, two girls, Patty and*
> *Sharon, sit on lawn chairs on a cool night and talk. Patty is blonde,*
> *Sharon brunette. They've been close friends since childhood, but Sharon*
> *is sometimes a bit cynical about the advantages Patty's beauty has*
> *brought her, and Patty has noticed that Sharon is "turning into a very*
> *bitter little person." But one thing Sharon seems to take pride in was*
> *that their friend Ben was in love with her one summer, when they spent*
> *a lot of time in the shade of a long alley of pomegranate trees by the*
> *playing fields. Patty is tired of Sharon patronizing her and decides to*
> *tell her what was really going on that summer.*

PATTY: Sharon, I touched him. This one evening, that summer, I touched him. Under the pomegranate trees. The sun was going down, and it was cool, under the pomegranate trees. And he'd been watching me all day, and we were sitting there, under the pomegranate trees. I was wearing my little yellow sundress. I looked really nice in that little sundress. He couldn't take his eyes off me. I could tell he was really aroused. You were on the other side of the field. Getting some ice cream from the creepy ice cream man or something. What was that song the ice cream truck played? Some really corny, ancient, grandma-type song. All that summer. And Ben was just crazy in love with me. I could see it. I could see how aroused he was. And I was fascinated by it. By the power I had. All this poor guy had to do was just look at me in my little yellow sundress, and all the blood in his body rushed right to his zipper. He couldn't help it. I felt this tremendous power over him. It was really intoxicating and also strangely touching. In fact, I was so moved at how much he must have wanted me at that moment, that I just sort of reached out my hand and touched him there. I didn't dream it. I touched him there. Under the pomegranate trees. And he looked at me while I was touching him, like he thought he was dreaming, and then his eyes closed, sort of like a dog when you scratch its stomach. And I knew he was mine forever. I could tell he'd never forget. As long as he lived, he'd never forget. Being there with me, under the pomegranate trees. "Strawberry Blonde." The song the ice cream man played. It was that really old song about the strawberry blonde. It was playing all the time I was touching him. He's never going to forget. Now that's power. Men don't have a very long attention span, ordinarily. But I'm the one he'll remember. I'm the strawberry blonde. *(Pause.)* It's getting cooler now. *(Pause.)* It feels nice. *(Pause.)* It gets cool all of a sudden in the desert. You think it's never going to be cool again, and suddenly there it is. It isn't much, but you'll take it. Love is like that. Like the relative coolness of the desert in the night. *(Pause.)* And things come out at night. Snakes and spiders and scorpions and all kinds of awful things. They're just waiting, during the day. During the heat of the day. And then at night they all scuttle out into the dark, to eat things and mate. Some of them mate first and then eat each other. It's really kind of horrible when you think about it. *(Pause.)*

Sharon? Are you crying? Did I make you cry? I didn't mean to make you cry. Honest to God I didn't. Please don't cry. I'm always doing that to people who love me, or people I love. But I don't mean to do it. I swear I don't. Sometimes a person just doesn't realize that they have power over people. The power to make them want you. The power to make them suffer. But if you're not used to feeling like you have any power, and then suddenly you discover that you've got it, it's just kind of, exhilarating, you know? But then it makes you sad afterwards. Like sex. It's just like sex. I could touch you. Would you like me to touch you? I could touch you, and then you'd always remember. You could close your eyes and remember. And imagine we're under the pomegranate trees.

THE VOWS OF PENELOPE CORELLI

Richard Vetere

Dramatic
Penelope, early fifties

> *Penelope is a woman living in Queens whose husband walked out on*
> *her five years ago. Since then she hit the lottery for fifty-three million*
> *dollars. Here she is speaking to her daughter, Sheila Maria, who has*
> *just told her that she wants to get married. Penelope is explaining to*
> *Sheila Maria how horrible her honeymoon was and, hence, her entire*
> *marriage.*

PENELOPE: Don't make me puke. I spent my honeymoon on Staten Island. Your father only had this dream to walk across one of the Great Big Lakes in the middle of winter. He saw some movie about some guy exploring the South Pole, and he and all his pals die in a tent with the wind howling outside the tent. Your father loved that movie. He loved how all the guys froze to death in the end. So, he wanted to walk across the lake, and so we planned to go to Chicago. In January. I wanted to go to Monte Carlo, but your father only had five hundred dollars on him. He had just hijacked a truck and that was his cut. A real Einstein your father. The plane can't take off because of a blizzard, so we take a cab to a motel in Staten Island, and we sit in the motel watching *I Love Lucy* reruns. That was my honeymoon. Then I had to go back to work the next week. Your father never got to walk across the lake. I think now, if I was with him there at this moment, I'd rip a hole in the ice and throw him in it!

THE VOWS OF PENELOPE CORELLI

Richard Vetere

Seriocomic
Sheila Maria, twenties

> *Sheila Maria's father walked out five years ago. She can't find a man to marry. Her mother has just hit the lottery for fifty-three million dollars. Here, she is speaking to Charlie Sunshine about how she thought he was courting her because he was interested in her, not because of her mother's newfound wealth.*

SHEILA: I thought you were here for me! Nobody ever comes here for me. I had to go to Sal's house when we were datin'. He never came here. I never got picked up here on a date — ever. The guys I dated always wanted to meet me at the off-ramp of the expressway! Then you show up with flowers, I thought, here at last! I told you that I couldn't sleep! It was because of you, Charlie Sunshine! I am ready to be loved, don't you see that! I thought I was ready at sixteen with Nicholas Walsh, but it was a false start! Now it's time I found who I loved and take them! But you — you're like concrete, you're like a brick wall — you just stand there and ignore my heart! A man should never ignore a woman's heart, Charlie! It's . . . it's what makes the universe spin! All the galaxies and star nebulas are nothing compared to the eternal mechanism of a woman's nucleus! If you ignore love . . . earthquakes will happen . . . tornadoes will blow . . . cyclones will explode, and your destiny will be blasted into the next century crippled by the lost opportunity of love! You lounge lizard! I got news for you. It's Motown that rocks my socks. Give me Marvin Gaye, Martha and the Vandellas, the Four Tops. Smokey Robinson. The Temptations! The Supremes!

THE VOWS OF PENELOPE CORELLI
Richard Vetere

Comic
Sheila Maria, twenties

Sheila Maria is telling her mother that she just saw her father, who left the house five years earlier and never came back. Despite her mother's very obvious disdain for her husband, Sheila Maria is beyond delighted to have her father back.

SHEILA: I saw Daddy! I saw my only father! On the Brooklyn Queens Expressway going over the Koskiusko Bridge coming down the Meeker Avenue off-ramp! I know it was him. I could see that majestic smile. I could see the wavy black hair turning a distinguished gray on the sides. I recognized his broad shoulders, the confidence beaming from his chest like a beacon of masculinity and daddyhood! His eyes cut through the invisible desert of urban life! His charm radiated through the four-lane blacktop of the American landscape! He shattered the Beaufort scale of wind force like a violent storm creating exceptionally high waves, uprooting trees, shaking loose chimney tops! The daddy of all daddies! An eight point eight on the Richter scale, a nine point oh on the Giuseppe Mercalli scale. A thirtyfold change in energy on the planet! A cirrocumulus cloud! Indicating an approaching storm! A hunter home from the hill — a sailor home from the sea. Sitting at the head of the table. Glorious, kingly, a master of the tribe, a mere mortal who has stolen fire from the gods! After years of an impossible journey, he has found his way back. He has fought the sheer brutality of bad luck and a terrible fate. He has rounded the bend, turned the curve, hit the runway, and filled an inside straight flush draw! He is here! My father is home!

THE WALL OF WATER
Sherry Kramer

Comic
Meg, twenties

Most of the monologues in The Wall of Water *are direct address and take place in New York, in the bathroom of the most wonderful apartment for the least rent in the world. As with most direct address, Meg speaks to the audience in an attempt to gain their sympathy — plead her case and get them on her side. Meg is the most recent of four roommates in this wonderful apartment. But this apartment has one fatal flaw: the lease is in Wendi's name, and Wendi is crazy. Really crazy. She is driving Meg nuts morning, noon, and night. Normally, Meg would stand up for herself, but she hasn't yet — she's a nice Midwesterner, and it's obvious that Wendi is sick. But it is dawning on Meg that while Wendi is sick, she is much more powerful than Meg — and that means Meg can strike back.*

MEG: I know what they want to talk to me about. WENDI. But I have nothing to apologize about when it comes to her. Day after day I have remembered that no matter what Wendi does to me, Wendi is sick. Wendi is weak. Day after day I have participated in absurd, tiny tragedies. I have even agreed on several occasions that the sky looked bruised. I have spent long nights pretending that everything that terrifies Wendi terrifies me too, but that I can handle it — hoping to help Wendi by my brave example. And I have spent even longer nights longing for any one of those terrifying things to come true. I would not mind, for example, if starting tomorrow the intestines of every woman wearing a red dress suddenly splashed out onto the ground, as long as Wendi was wearing one. I would also not object, for instance, if every sound that has ever been made since the Earth's surface cooled, sounds from the past ten or twenty billion years or so, suddenly reversed their journey out to the stars and returned in a deafening barrage that made conversation impossible and was just barely survivable by the population at large, as long as Wendi does indeed have hearing as sensitive and delicate as if she had dog ears, a fact she is constantly reminding me of whenever I am having a normal conversation in my room that she cannot possibly hear or playing my stereo at barely audible levels . . .

(She has been raving for several moments — she gets a hold of herself.)

. . . Excuse me. I would not mind the end of life as we know it and the loss of the known world, as long as Wendi was lost with it. I suspect that this is not healthy for me . . . So, assuming that the dirty dishes in the sink are not going to grow teeth during the night and eat her, I have to face this problem myself. I have to face the fact that I can't go on like this. I have to face the fact that I must fight back. Wendi is stomping on me. I must stomp back. And, since I would never stomp on anybody weaker than I am, I have to face the fact that Wendi is, in reality, stronger than I am.

(She realizes it's true!) Yes — *Of course she is. It's obvious, isn't it? The evidence is everywhere. Wendi is stronger than I am.* She's got me giving up cigarettes, doesn't she, a thing I love. A thing I love to do at the risk of throat cancer and head cancer and lung cancer, the three most hideous ways that cancer comes. She is the one who is stronger. And everybody knows that while you aren't allowed to stomp on anybody weaker than you are, you are actually encouraged to stomp on anybody stronger if you dare. WENDI! WENDI!!! WENDI, I AM GOING TO KILL YOU!

THE WALL OF WATER
Sherry Kramer

Comic
Denice, twenties

> *Denice is a drop-dead gorgeous party girl on a first date with Dr. Gig
> Hollis, an odd, lumpy, egomaniacal psychiatrist. Denice has disguised
> herself as one of her roommates: Dr. Judy Wilson, a dowdy, dead-
> serious, egomaniacal allergist. Denice is on this date because she wants
> a picture of Dr. Hollis for her scrapbook — an odd obsession, but one
> to which she is devoted. Denice is a smart party girl. She has many de-
> grees, including several Ph.Ds, so when Gig asks her to tell him about
> her research, she has no problem making this up.*

DENICE: I fear for the children of the parents of free love, casual sex, and multiple, meaningful, brief encounters. Assume that both the mother and
father of these children have had twenty sexual partners each prior to
marriage. Then consider that each of those forty partners has slept with
twenty people each themselves. Well, those eight hundred people have
slept with sixteen thousand people. Those sixteen thousand have slept
with three hundred and twenty thousand. And those three hundred and
twenty thousand have slept with a total of six million four hundred
thousand people each. So when the next generation has children — or
tries to — even if they have slept with only one partner each — their off-
spring will carry the combined weight of one hundred and twenty-eight
million allergic reactions traced in the DNA of their blood and skin and
bones. So the next time you see a particularly unattractive, sexually and
emotionally repulsive person — someone who could manage one or two
sexual contacts at best — look again. You may be looking at the future
of mankind. For soon, only the descendants of the ugly, the hideously
stupid, and the obscenely obese will be left to walk the earth. To lie
down together, in the dark and procreate.

But enough about me.

WHAT SHALL I DO FOR PRETTY GIRLS?

Don Nigro

Dramatic
Georgie, forties

> *Georgie, the wife of the great Irish poet William Butler Yeats, married Yeats when he was reeling from repeated rejections by both his longtime love Maud Gonne and Maud's beautiful daughter, Iseult. Georgie has managed to keep her husband's attention by faking visitations from the spirit world that have given him metaphors for some of his greatest poetry, but in her heart, she's always known that he still loves Maud and Iseult in a way he's never felt about her. Now, after twenty years of marriage, Georgie confronts him about his persistent love for Maud and Iseult.*

GEORGIE: I have two remarkable children and a good life, and I value what I have. But I'm greedy. I want more. I want to be loved the way you loved that crazy woman and her whore of a daughter. What is it about such women that makes men love them? Are men so stupid they can't see past the way a woman looks — or looked once, in the case of the old one — to what's empty and dead inside? They're dead, Willy. Their souls are dead. The one's destroyed her soul with politics and hate and the other by giving herself to a vicious pig and liking it. Well, I am not anybody's damned muse, Willy. I am a real woman. I have a mind and a soul and a heart, and I'm strong and brave and smart and stubborn and a good mother and a good wife and a good friend, and I have loved you like nobody else ever has. And it means nothing to you. It means nothing. Nobody has felt for anybody what you've felt for those women. You don't even know what you've felt for those women. They aren't women at all. They're somebody in your head. I think they were in your head before you ever met them. I can't compete with that. Nobody can compete with that. I could make up a thousand talking spooks for the rest of my life and none of it would make up for that. Before long, you'll be old and sick, and then I'll take care of you. Then you'll be mine. Then you'll be all mine. Or at least that's what I'll tell myself.

WHAT SHALL I DO FOR PRETTY GIRLS?

Don Nigro

Seriocomic
Maud, late forties

> *In the summer of 1917, Maud Gonne, once a great beauty and still an imposing woman and a lightning rod of Irish political struggle for many years, speaks to her friend, the great Irish poet William Butler Yeats, in her house in Normandy. Maud, whose husband was executed in the Irish rebellion, is a widow, and Yeats, her suitor for many years, has made the dangerous journey over the channel in wartime to dutifully propose to her again. She's just refused him again, somewhat to his relief, and then suggested that perhaps he should marry her beautiful but troubled daughter Iseult. Yeats has responded that he doesn't think Iseult considers him marriage material and doesn't know anything about women.*

MAUD: Don't be coy, Willy. You've bedded your share. Florence Farr. Olivia Shakespeare. That very strange Mabel person. It took you a while to get started, but you've been doing a good job catching up, now that you've figured out that a woman will sleep with a poet now and again as long as he's in love with somebody else. Perhaps my daughter aspires to make an appearance in the index to your biography. And don't tell me you don't fancy her. I've seen the way you look at her. She's an odd duck, is what she is. But you've always been reduced to dribbling idiocy by beauty. She's led a sheltered and disorderly life. My fault entirely. And now we spend our nights sitting in the parlor listening to the naval bombardment and hoping a stray shell doesn't reduce us to unrecognizable fragments. The house shakes like a wet dog. We've been dining on torpedoed fish that wash up on shore, and on the pale and emaciated products of our wretched garden. It's a bizarre life I've given her. I once thought war was a noble thing. I've seen it close up now, and it's all vanity in a slaughterhouse. How shameful that I ever thought like a man. It was brave of you to cross the channel. You might have been sunk or blown up.

We are both servants to the young goddess. So proposing to me was just an afterthought. No, don't blather your halfhearted denials at me. You knew you'd be expected to. You asked me. I said no. We've played our scene. I expect she wants to torture you some more. But you can't actually marry her, of course. I was forgetting she's your daughter.

SCENES

ALIENS WITH EXTRAORDINARY SKILLS

Saviana Stanescu

Seriocomic
Nadia, twenties
Lupita, late twenties

> *Nadia, an illegal immigrant from Moldova, works as a clown, making money by twisting balloons and doing tricks at McDonald's. Her room-mate, Lupita, is a Dominican American and a professional exotic dancer. Here, Nadia begs Lupita to let her go to a party in Soho to pro-vide the entertainment, as she doesn't have enough money to pay the rent. (Note: A slash [/] indicates overlapping dialogue.)*

(Around six P.M., Lupita's and Nadia's apartment. A fancy shoebox is on the sofa. Balloon toys are on the floor. Lupita tries on a pair of shoes and walks around the living room. Nadia has just finished making a balloon horse.)

NADIA: Columbus Circle is a good spot. I like it there. It near the park and I can just stand by the statue and twist balloons. Squirrels sell the best. Five bucks. Dogs are the cheapest: only two bucks. It easy to make them. Horses are three bucks. They're actually dogs with longer neck. I made one hundred ninety dollars last week and one hundred seventy-five the week before.

LUPITA: It doesn't seem like a good spot. *(Kicking a balloon animal.)* This liv-ing room has turned into a rubber zoo. You'd make more money twist-ing condoms!

(They laugh. Nadia crams the balloon animals under the sofa. She looks at Lupita with admiration.)

NADIA: Are they really Manolo Blahnik?

LUPITA: Of course. What kinda silly question is that? Look at the label. I paid seven hundred twenty-five bucks for them.

NADIA: Wow.

LUPITA: Yeah. My tips for a week.

NADIA: That . . . lots of money.

LUPITA: I deserve them. I work hard.

NADIA: You look gorgeous.

LUPITA: I must. *(Beat.)* Hey, wanna try them on?

NADIA: They're yours, I can't . . .

LUPITA: C'mon, try them on, we have the same size!

NADIA: *(Excited.)* OK!

(She tries them on and walks the way Lupita did.)

NADIA: I will never afford such shoes.

LUPITA: Never say never, sis. You gotta work on your self-esteem and the success will come. When you look in the mirror, what do you tell yourself?

NADIA: Nothing.

LUPITA: You gotta talk to yourself, honey. Stuff like: I'm gonna make it, I know I'm gonna make it. I will . . . such and such, whatever you dream to be. Working on your self-esteem, hon, that the way to go.

NADIA: But I do have self-esteem. I like what I do. I only need to make more money.

LUPITA: Don't forget your rent is due on Monday. I mean, I'm cool and nice, I like you and all that, but you gotta pay the rent on time, honey. I don't run a charity business here.

NADIA: I will pay. I will work hard this weekend, I will.

LUPITA: You mean you don't have the money?

NADIA: Not yet.

LUPITA: And how exactly do you plan to find work?

NADIA: This weekend I'll dress as a clown and go to the McDonald's in Harlem. I'll make tricks for the kids. I'll pass the hat . . . I'm sure I'll get hired for some birthday parties. I'm cheap, for eighty dollars they get lots of fun out of me.

LUPITA: You won't make the seven hundred fifty for the rent then.

NADIA: I will. I will work the whole weekend.

LUPITA: Girl, I'm sorry to sound like a bitch, but you won't make that kinda money doing tricks for some kids at McDonald's. You gotta find some rich clients, you gotta be invited to the Upper West Side or Long Island. That's where you make money, not in Central Park.

(Nadia takes the shoes off.)

LUPITA: Put them in the box.

(Nadia puts the shoes in the box.)

LUPITA: Look, me, I got three gigs on Friday night, and Friday is my big money night at the club with three of my big clients plus my new regular — a silly guy from "Tennessee." So I can't take this gig at a party in Soho where a friend recommended me.

NADIA: I can go in your place! Can I go in your place?

LUPITA: It an adults-only party.

NADIA: I can create new tricks for adults. All adults have an inner child.

LUPITA: Girl . . . You're not right for this gig. You haven't done this kinda stuff before. OK, it's no sex involved and no stripping, but you might have to slap a hand or two that gropes your ass, you know.

NADIA: You haven't seen me working; I'm really tough when it comes to work.

LUPITA: I dunno . . . If you go, you gotta keep your wits about you. You gotta be careful. Don't drink no shit they give you.

NADIA: I come from a country with heavy vodka drinkers . . .

LUPITA: I dunno . . . You will freak out when some sweaty guy shouts: C'mon, shake it, baby, shake it!

NADIA: I can shake it, I can. *(She starts swaying her body in a sexy way; she's funny rather than sexy.)*

LUPITA: You're as sexy as a pumpkin . . . *(She gets up and starts moving in a very sexy way.)* See, you gotta sway your hips like this!

NADIA: *(Moving better.)* Look! I can do it!

LUPITA: *(Sitting.)* You're a clown. Stick to that, girl.

NADIA: Please, Lupi! Just this time, get me this gig! Those people might have kids; they'll see what I can do and invite me to kid parties. I'm very good, they will like me, you'll / see!

LUPITA: I don't like this. You gotta figure out a way to make money to pay your rent. You can't rely on me to help with that. I work hard to pay my bills *on time*. Last year I was short on money, and I got an eviction notice. I can't let that happen anymore. I took the job at the club, and I was never late on rent ever since.

NADIA: I'm sorry . . . I / will (find a way to pay) . . .

LUPITA: They sent the "five-day notice" seven times, in English and Spanish. It scared the shit outta me. This is a tough city, you know.

NADIA: I know.

LUPITA: No, you don't. Do you know why I'm renting the living room?

NADIA: For money?

LUPITA: I'm renting the living room so I can work at the club only until midnight instead of two A.M. I'm renting the living room to save money for acting classes.

NADIA: Then let me go to this party! I have to make money. I won't ask for any other gigs. Please, please. Only this time. I promise / I will . . .

LUPITA: OK, OK . . . Calm down. *(Beat.)* I guess it can't be too bad. Soho people are classy: middle-aged businessmen and older artsy guys who like fancy food and exotic dancers . . . There was this belly dancer from Morocco, Isset, they worshipped her. She ended up with a divorced lawyer in his late fifties who got her a house in the Hamptons and now she's sorta running his "bed breakfast" . . . (*Lupita laughs. Nadia is relieved; she laughs too.*) Maybe you'll find your Mr. Big over there.

NADIA: My Mr. Big should be a perfect gentleman. Totally in love with me. Making coffee for both of us in the morning. The most perfect coffee in the world. Not too sweet, not too strong. Just the way I like it . . .

LUPITA: There's plenty of Starbucks boys.

(*They laugh.*)

AMERICAN TET
Lydia Stryk

Dramatic
Amy Krombacher, midtwenties.
Elaine Krombacher, midfifties.

> *Amy lives at home and is putting herself through college by working on the*
> *local military base. Elaine, Amy's mother, is a career military wife who cur-*
> *rently teaches new spouses the ins and outs of military life on base. It is the*
> *spring of 2004, the one-year anniversary of the ongoing conflagration in*
> *Iraq. Amy is beginning to bring home stories of unhappiness and misfortune*
> *on base from other military family members involved in Iraq, reporting on*
> *coworkers affected by the war as a way to begin confiding her own depres-*
> *sion and emerging antiwar feelings to her mother. Elaine feels attacked by*
> *Amy's anger and is fearful of her radical views. She is determined to defend*
> *her way of life. Both their thoughts, meanwhile, are on Danny, Amy's*
> *brother, who is coming home on leave from Iraq soon. Elaine is determined*
> *to focus on the party she is planning for him. Amy fears for his life.*

(The backyard. Amy and Elaine.)

AMY: She can't stop eating. She's OK 'til she starts. So she has breakfast for
  dinner. But it doesn't really help. 'Cause then she stays up all night. Eating. She's just exhausted all the time. Wendy's started drinking. Cheap
  port wine, mostly. Can't get out of bed sometimes. She calls in sick. And
  me . . . I'm just . . .

ELAINE: You're just what . . . ?

AMY: I'm just gonna hurt someone.

ELAINE: Amy?

AMY: It's like bombs are going off. Inside of me.

ELAINE: Honey. *(A difficult pause.)* I know this war on terror isn't easy.

AMY: Who's spreading the terror?

ELAINE: Amy.

AMY: Answer.

ELAINE: Well, we're fighting for peace and serenity. Over there. If that's what
  you mean. *(Pause.)* We brought freedom. To the Iraqis. *(Pause.)* And

we'll keep spreading it everywhere. Everywhere. Everywhere necessary. Until we've won. And the war on terror is over. And there's peace.

AMY: What's gonna happen when it never comes? Then we bomb again? Just keep on? Bombing. Bombing. Bomb —

ELAINE: Shh! *Stop . . .* stop. It'll be OK. We just have to trust in what our leaders say. It'll be —

AMY: Trust *who?* When all we hear is lies?

ELAINE: Oh, honey. *(A pause.)* On a brighter note, we stopped those Taliban.

AMY: The Taliban have not gone away.

ELAINE: We certainly tried.

AMY: We funded them.

ELAINE: Should we have let the Afghanis fall to communism?

AMY: If it were my choice, I'd have taken communism.

ELAINE: *(Aghast, looking around to make sure no one has heard this, in a whisper.) Communism?*

AMY: Yes, Mom. *(Shouting.)* COMMUNISM!!! COMMUNISM ROCKS!!! *(Elaine gets up.)*

ELAINE: Amy, I don't think that's funny. Your father put his life on the line to bring communism down. And he almost lost it. And he is not well now. And thousands died. But we won, thank God.

AMY: We were fighting the wrong enemy.

ELAINE: We'll never get it perfect, Amy. *(Pause.)* If your dad could hear you.

AMY: He doesn't listen to me, anyway. He thinks I'm crazy.

ELAINE: That's not true.

AMY: Don't lie to me.

ELAINE: OK. He thinks you're crazy.

(A pause. Amy and Elaine laugh. The air seems to clear.)

AMY: Communism was not the enemy is all I am trying to say. And terrorism isn't either.

ELAINE: *(Holding her chest.) Terrorism* isn't the enemy either? Terrorism isn't — ! — the enemy. *(Slowly.)* OK. And who *is* the enemy, Amy?

AMY: The enemy's inside, Mom.

(Elaine looks toward the house, confused, dismayed.)

AMY: Inside of us. *(Pointing her finger to her head like a gun.)* In here. The enemy's in our heads, Mom. It's ignorance.

ELAINE: *(Exasperated now, finally turning on her.)* This is not a pretty world, missy. You have to stand for something. If they win, we lose. Is that what you want to happen? Do you want to live in their world?

(Amy doesn't answer; she looks away.)

ELAINE: Well, do you?

(Amy does not respond.)

ELAINE: *(Shouting the question.) Do you???* This is my world, Amy. And I'm looking around it. And it's not so bad. This is *our world.* You couldn't say those things in China. You couldn't wear those clothes in Iran. You'd be covered in a veil with slits for eyes. You couldn't even drive. You do not know, little girl, how lucky you are, how lucky. To wake up in this land, free. You'd be married off by age six. You'd be locked in a dungeon with that mouth of yours. You'd never even see the inside of a school. But freedom isn't free. Someone's got to pay. This is not a pretty world. You've got to stand for something. I am so proud of my country. I'm so proud and grateful. I pray for it every day, and I know you think that's crazy. The tired and the poor from the world over, they want to get here. No matter what they say. Everyone wants to be an American. Everyone wants what we have. This is paradise, honey. These are sacred shores. You wake up free, little girl. Do you know what that means? These terrorists. They hate us because they hate freedom. If they win. We lose. Is that what you want to happen? Do you really want to live in their world? Do you, Amy?

AMY: It's one world, Mom. And it's going up in flames.

(A pause. Elaine looks at Amy. She seems to be about to answer. She sighs. She looks around the yard, studying it.)

ELAINE: We're going to need a lot of balloons. And a big old "Welcome Home" sign . . .

(Amy looks at her mother, shakes her head. She gets up, slowly.)

AMY: Danny's going to die. *(She leaves.)*

ELAINE: A big old "Welcome Home" sign. Or paper cutout letters . . .

AUGUST IS A THIN GIRL
Julie Marie Myatt

Dramatic
Eve, early thirties
Belinda, twenty

> *Eve is a rather mysterious woman on the run from something. She has stopped at a motel in Idaho, where she has met Belinda, a local woman with a husband and two kids who works at the motel.*

> *(Inside the motel room. Morning. Belinda enters with cleaning supplies. She's hungover and slow. She begins to strip the bed. Eve exits from the bathroom in a towel.)*

BELINDA: Check out's at noon, you know.

EVE: I know.

BELINDA: Are you one of those . . . one of those . . . what do you call them . . . nudist?

EVE: No.

BELINDA: How come you're always naked?

EVE: Because you never knock. *(She laughs.)*

BELINDA: Whatever.

EVE: It's still my room.

BELINDA: I thought you'd be gone.

EVE: I've got plenty of time —

BELINDA: Yeah, well, don't pussyfoot around. I've got a lot of rooms to clean. Damn 4-H club checked out this morning and left the place a fucking pig sty. Freaks.

EVE: Why don't you go clean those rooms and let me take a shower?

BELINDA: I always start this side of the building.

EVE: Start on the other side.

> *(Belinda plops on the bed.)*

BELINDA: I feel like shit. I wish I could throw up. I hate this job.

EVE: Look, I am trying to get out of here. If you'll let me shower —

BELINDA: You do kind of smell . . . Smells like sex.

EVE: I don't think so — *(She laughs.)*

BELINDA: Yep, that's what it is.

EVE: No —

BELINDA: I can sniff out every single thing that goes on in this place. So don't tell me that's not sex. This nose is a fucking ace detective. I walk into a room and I know. Instantly. Perfume is a dead giveaway — Be careful, Jovan musk is like a fucking bull's-eye — Aftershave. Baby powder. Baby shit. Dogs. Cats. Ferrets. Booze. Cheese curls. You name it. Things I wish I'd never smelled.

EVE: You're wrong about this —

BELINDA: Look at the bed. Both sides are messy. Did you do that yourself?

EVE: Yes.

BELINDA: Bullshit.

EVE: Restless night.

BELINDA: Uh-huh.

EVE: I've got a long day ahead of me —

BELINDA: Should have got an early start then, huh?

EVE: I'm trying.

BELINDA: Doesn't look like it. Books open. Clothes are half packed. Shoes are over there. Bed's warm.

EVE: It's still early —

BELINDA: Too fucking early. Damn owner thinks we Americans like to work at the break of dawn. That shit might fly in Korea, but I'm in no hurry to get on my hands and knees to clean up semen stains and redneck vomit. *(She gets up.)* There's not enough Mr. Clean in the world for that shit. I swear I'm lucky I don't go fucking crazy from all the things I've seen in this place. You wouldn't believe — people don't give a flying fuck what they do outside their own homes. Who has to clean it up. Disgusting people traveling this country. Freaks. Animals most of them. *(She grabs her cleaning supplies.)* But, looks like your company was decent. Little beer, little food . . . nothing was broken. One-night stand, huh?

EVE: No.

BELINDA: Did he rough you up?

EVE: What?

BELINDA: All those bruises.

EVE: No —

BELINDA: Where'd you meet him?

EVE: I didn't have a one-night —

BELINDA: I could use one of those. What's his name?

EVE: I don't know anyone here. How could I have a one-night stand?

BELINDA: Easy. The men are so hard up in this town all you have to do is spit at them and they'll come in their pants. *(She heads for the door.)* But looks like you already found that out. *(She picks up one of the beer bottles.)* It wasn't my husband, was it?

EVE: He was with you.

BELINDA: Oh yeah . . . that's right. I guess I should go clean twenty-nine first. Get that puke before it dries.

EVE: Uh-huh.

BELINDA: I told him he had too much. He won't stop until the whole box is gone. Idiot. *(She sees the empty pill bottle and pen on the dresser on the way out. Picks up both. Studies the pill bottle first.)* Hello. What are these?

EVE: They're gone.

BELINDA: What were they? Anything good?

EVE: No.

BELINDA: I could use a party. Something to blow my fucking mind right out of my head.

EVE: Those wouldn't do that.

BELINDA: What would they do?

EVE: Prevent it.

BELINDA: Prevent what?

EVE: Mind blowing — *(She throws down the bottle.)*

BELINDA: Hap's Chevron. You get a fill up there?

EVE: Uh. Yeah.

(Belinda clicks the pen and looks around the room.)

BELINDA: Uh-huh . . . looks like that's not all you got.

EVE: I got the pen. *(She laughs.)*

BELINDA: And a freak to go with it?

EVE: I'd like to take a shower.

BELINDA: Did he blow your mind?

EVE: I'd like to take a shower —

BELINDA: Well, well, well. Looks like there's a new girl on the block, huh?

EVE: No.

BELINDA: Rounding up the bad boys. *(She opens the door.)* I better be careful. *(Belinda throws the pen to Eve.)* You could be the talk of the town. *(She exits.)*

BECKY SHAW
Gina Gionfriddo

Dramatic
Becky, thirty-four
Andrew, thirty-one

> *Becky and Andrew have been coworkers for about a month. Becky is a*
> *temp in the law office where Andrew, a frustrated would-be novelist, is*
> *the office manager. Andrew is a newlywed whose wife, Suzanna, asked*
> *him to fix up her adopted brother and best friend Max with an eligible*
> *woman. So Andrew introduced Becky and Max, and they had one date*
> *— a few days before this scene — during which they were mugged at*
> *gunpoint. In this scene, Andrew has just arrived at Becky's apartment in*
> *response to a call from her saying that she's heard a noise and feels afraid.*

> *(Andrew and Becky in Becky's apartment the following night. Andrew has*
> *brought beer and a pizza.)*

BECKY: I'm so sorry. I heard this weird noise and since the holdup, I'm just
. . . *(Indicates jittery.)*

ANDREW: It's totally OK.

BECKY: But to make you come running over here . . . Suzanna must hate me.

ANDREW: No. It's good I got out of the house. She's . . . studying.

BECKY: Please thank her for speaking with Max on my behalf.

ANDREW: Not that it helped.

BECKY: What did he say — exactly?

ANDREW: A lot of bullshit that has nothing to do with you.

BECKY: Really? If he thinks I'm a loser, I can take it. It's the silence that's so
awful . . .

ANDREW: It's not that.

BECKY: So what is it?

ANDREW: I think he just can't deal with what happened. He's emotionally
a very . . . stunted man.

BECKY: Then why did you set me up with him?
(Awkward beat.)

ANDREW: I'd met him twice before that night. I trusted Susie . . .

BECKY: Max wasn't at your wedding?

ANDREW: No . . . We got married kind of fast. In Las Vegas.

BECKY: Why so fast?

ANDREW: It was just a really intense time.

BECKY: How was it intense?

ANDREW: Susie's life was just . . . It was seriously, the most epic, Faulknerian chaos I've ever encountered outside a fictional paradigm. *(Pause.)* Did I just sound like a total tool?

BECKY: No, I understand.

ANDREW: Susie's dad had just died. We met on a ski trip and she was so sad. Susie's little, you know, and she wore this red parka. I would look at her against these huge, white mountains and think . . . I shouldn't tell you, it's weird.

BECKY: Tell me.

ANDREW: I would look at her and think . . . She's like blood on the snow. Her sadness is wrong, and I want to fix it.

BECKY: I don't think that's weird. You were falling in love.

ANDREW: Sure felt like it. It makes more sense if you knew her then. She was really different. More . . . delicate.

BECKY: Suzanna? That's hard to imagine.

ANDREW: Oh, I know. She's so much healthier now.

BECKY: She's lucky she found you.

ANDREW: *(After a beat.)* Look, I want to apologize. Susie is blind to Max's flaws, but I —

BECKY: He takes such good care of her.

ANDREW: Well . . . They're family. And on paper, Max looks great. He's rich, charismatic, looking to settle down —

BECKY: He's looking to settle down? He said that?

ANDREW: He told Susie, you know, "I'm thirty-six; I'm ready to . . . *(Thinking.)* to, I guess be open. . ."

BECKY: Wow. I kind of wish you hadn't told me that.

ANDREW: Saying it is one thing. He's never gonna do it.

BECKY: Wait. You fixed me up with someone you think is never going to settle down?

ANDREW: No, no, no —

BECKY: He said he wants to settle down and he meant it, right? You're just trying to save my feelings now by lying —

ANDREW: I'm not lying. I just found out. *(Pause.)* Look. Susie wasn't studying when you called. We were fighting because Susie said that Max is . . . a short-timer.

BECKY: What is a "short-timer"?

ANDREW: It's a Vietnam War term. It means guys who go into combat for short stints and don't stay. Max, apparently, only dates women for, like, three months.

BECKY: Oh.

ANDREW: I didn't know that until tonight. Susie said it and I just flipped —

BECKY: She should have told you.

ANDREW: I know. And I wasn't gonna tell you, but then you got so upset about the . . . Max-settling-down thing . . .

BECKY: *(Covers her eyes, tears up.)* I'm sorry. *(Cries/gasps.)* Oh, my God, Andrew. It hurts!

ANDREW: You know what? *(Takes her hands in his.)* Tell me what hurts.

BECKY: I had a gun pointed at me!

ANDREW: So it's the gun . . .

BECKY: He was black. And that hurts me! Because I was hurt very badly . . . twice. It's why I don't talk to my parents . . .

ANDREW: A black man . . . hurt you? It's OK. It's OK. Tell me how he hurt you.

BECKY: When I was a freshman at Brown I met a boy who really liked me. He was black . . . And my parents said, you know, it's him or it's us. Choose.

ANDREW: Are you serious?

BECKY: And I couldn't face losing my family. So I ended it with Stefan, and I learned after I let him go that he had truly loved me and my family didn't. I tried to go backwards. But he wouldn't . . . I had kind of a breakdown. I had a scholarship and I lost it.

ANDREW: Shit. I'm sorry.

BECKY: Then . . . Last year, I was working at a law firm and I became involved with one of the lawyers who was — is — black. I told him that if I committed to him, I would lose my family, so he had to be very sure he wanted me . . .

ANDREW: He wasn't sure. . .

BECKY: No, he was. I cut ties with my family. I moved into his house. He has a house . . . on the water in Cranston. I was so happy! Then he changed his mind.

ANDREW: Oh, shit.

BECKY: I've been having these terrible racist feelings since the holdup. I've been thinking that black men have ruined my life and I . . . I can't say it.

ANDREW: Say it. Say anything. I told you my blood-on-the-snow thing. Come on . . .

BECKY: Walking to the bus, I get pictures in my mind of black men . . . being tortured . . . God, I fucking hate myself!

ANDREW: Becky, you had a trauma. You're allowed to feel some crazy shit for a while. And you're not gonna act on these thoughts, right? You're small, but you're intense . . .

BECKY: Don't say I'm intense! Jason said that when he left me.

ANDREW: It's not a bad thing.

BECKY: Yes, it is. Men don't want intense women.

ANDREW: Uh . . . Yeah, we do.

BECKY: You think you do, but you don't. Jason left me. You're fighting with Suzanna . . .

ANDREW: We'll get past it. Look. Intensity is a good thing. It means you can love. It's just a matter of, you know, how you channel it.

BECKY: I can see where Suzanna might lash out and that would be so much healthier . . .

ANDREW: Healthier for her, maybe.

BECKY: Sometimes the fantasy isn't enough and I think about cutting myself with a knife.

ANDREW: *(Rallying.)* Then we need to go to the hospital. Tonight.

BECKY: I don't have insurance.

ANDREW: I don't care. If you want to hurt yourself, I have to protect you.

BECKY: I feel that. I feel safe with you. It's wonderful. To feel safe. This is starting to feel a little . . . intimate.

ANDREW: Do you have any girlfriends? Maybe you could call . . .

BECKY: I lost them when I moved in with Jason.

ANDREW: Wow. Your friends were all racists?

BECKY: They weren't racist at all, actually. It's just . . . Jason made me happy and happiness made me mean. To women. Not to Jason.

ANDREW: What did you do?

BECKY: Dumped them. You know the all-female table in the bar? Women drinking fucking Midori sours pretending to like each other while they scan for men.

ANDREW: God, I can't stand women like that . . .

BECKY: But I am women like that! I got a boyfriend and I dumped all my friends! *(Surveying the room.)* Maybe this is my punishment, you know?

ANDREW: The holdup?

BECKY: No. This. Back to the studio apartment and the secretary table at happy hour. *(After a beat.)* If not for the holdup, Andrew . . . I think Max and I . . . I think it could have worked.

ANDREW: No —

BECKY: You're an honest person. When you told me Max was coarse on the outside and rich inside . . . Andrew, I saw that in him.

ANDREW: No. Becky . . . Forget that. Forget him.

BECKY: Andrew, we slept together.

ANDREW: You . . . So he did call you.

BECKY: No. I'm so embarrassed. We slept together that night.

ANDREW: After the . . . robbery?

BECKY: After the police station, we wanted a drink to calm down. But nothing was open. So we went to his hotel.

ANDREW: You went to Boston?

BECKY: No. He had rented a room here for the night.

ANDREW: He rented a room in advance? Are you kidding me?

BECKY: We had some drinks and . . . It turned kind of bad.

ANDREW: Did he hurt you?

BECKY: Not . . . sexually. He just wouldn't let me stay overnight.

ANDREW: He what?

BECKY: He gave me cab fare . . .

ANDREW: Cab fare?

BECKY: I told him I didn't want to be alone after what had happened, and he offered me his credit card to get my own room in the hotel.

ANDREW: Let me get this straight. He fucked you —

BECKY: Please don't say that.

ANDREW: He had sex with you, he kicked you out of his bed, and he offered you money.

BECKY: Not for sex! For a hotel or a cab. In his way, he was taking care of me.

ANDREW: No. Becky, he's sick! Listen: I will take care of you. You are never to contact him again. Do you hear me?

BECKY: Yes. I hear you. Yes.

BECKY SHAW
Gina Gionfriddo

Dramatic
Max, thirty-six
Suzanna, thirty-five

> *Max, a wealthy self-made money manager, was "kind of adopted" by Suzanna's family when he was ten. Suzanna refers to him as "my brother" in conversations with her new husband, Andrew, but their relationship has been fraught with sexual tension since their teen years, and they had sex on one occasion, a year before this scene. Here, Suzanna takes Max to task for his conduct after a blind date she and Andrew set up for him.*

(Max and Suzanna in Max's hotel room in Boston.)

SUZANNA: You shouldn't have slept with her, Max.

MAX: She initiated it!

SUZANNA: I don't care. You knew you didn't want to see her again, and she'd just been held up with a gun . . .

MAX: She initiated it!

SUZANNA: I don't care. It was selfish and sleazy.

MAX: She grabbed me like this. (*He demonstrates on Suzanna.*) She said, "I need this."

SUZANNA: You kicked her out of bed afterwards!

MAX: Oh, come on. I didn't stay in your bed after we . . . did it. I have a sleep disorder!

SUZANNA: No, Max. You have an intimacy issue that you pay a doctor to call a sleep disorder.

MAX: Are you a doctor? Have you seen my sleep study?

SUZANNA: Fuck your sleep study. Having sex and then leaving . . . or kicking out . . . it's degrading. You need to get some sleeping pills.

MAX: You think I haven't tried that? They give me a hangover.

SUZANNA: Love, Max, is worth a hangover.

MAX: Do you understand the pressure of my job? I'm not a . . . a barista . . . poet . . . secretary boy like Andrew. I control people's money. I can't be off my game!

SUZANNA: So your clients matter and your women don't?

MAX: Uhhh . . . If you're asking me will I jeopardize people's life savings because women need to cuddle, the answer is no.

SUZANNA: *(After a beat.)* Call Becky Shaw. Call her now.

MAX: No!

SUZANNA: She says she's suicidal, Max. Andrew is afraid to leave her alone. I've barely seen him since this happened.

MAX: That's Andrew's bad, not mine. You pulled that suicidal shit with me, I didn't come running.

SUZANNA: Hence me marrying Andrew and not you.

(A hard silence, then a spike in anger for both.)

MAX: Say what you want, but give me credit. I cured you. And I did it by refusing to enable the Sylvia Plath, postcollegiate bullshit —

SUZANNA: You cured me? No. Meeting Andrew cured me.

MAX: Yeah? Well, you met Andrew because I kicked your ass. I kicked your ass out of bed and onto that fucking ski trip!

(A beat. He's right.)

SUZANNA: And I am so, so grateful. Are you trying to torpedo my marriage? If you are, please stop.

MAX: Jesus, Suzanna. You let a crazy woman into your life. You let her into mine. How have I become the bad guy?

SUZANNA: Because you won't help me! That's what loving someone is, Max. It's doing stuff you don't want to do. It's staying in bed all night. It's listening when you can't help. And right now . . . today . . . this minute . . . It is calling Becky Fucking Shaw so I can get my husband back!

(Her level of distress surprises and affects Max. He takes it in and then . . . a gentleness to his approach.)

MAX: OK, calm down. Go back to Providence. I'll call her.

SUZANNA: Thank you, Max. Thank you.

MAX: I'm also gonna give you some advice. Your husband is not the fucking Red Cross. The last time he started consoling a cute, suicidal chick, he married her. He hears, "I want to hurt myself" like a fucking mating call.

SUZANNA: No . . .

MAX: Yes . . .

SUZANNA: Just make her go away.

(Max genuinely wants to ease Suzanna's pain. But the notion of Suzanna's marriage imploding is undeniably appealing, too.)

BRAINPEOPLE
José Rivera

Dramatic
Ani, thirties
Mayannah, thirties

> *Mayannah, a wealthy, possibly disturbed heiress of Puerto Rican descent, is hosting a dinner party at her mansion in Los Angeles. She has invited two total strangers: Ani, an Armenian woman, who is smart, almost pathologically lonely, and very peculiar, and Rosemary, who suffers from multiple personality disorder. Rosemary has just left the room, giving Mayannah and Ani time to talk. In this scene, it appears that they have something in common.*

ANI: Holy Jesus — a total one-woman circus just walked out of this room!

MAYANNAH: But don't you get it, Ani — she's so *porous* — oh God, *this could be the night!*

ANI: Mayannnah, it's been — *wow*. Truly. But, you know, between the sirens and the tiger meat and Sybil in the next room . . . you need to tell your driver to take me home.

MAYANNAH: Home? What?

ANI: Yes. I don't care about the curfew. Or how many points they're going to take from me.

MAYANNAH: But you haven't touched your food. That's part of the deal. At least have the tiger meat —

ANI: But I don't even know why I'm here. Maybe this was all a mistake. I don't care how much money you're giving me. I'll find another way to leave this country!

MAYANNAH: Ani! Do you know how much I paid those hunters to track down this tiger? The number of embassies I bribed to get the carcass into my kitchen?

ANI: Too bad I don't seem to care.

MAYANNAH: But it's my anniversary dinner. The most important night of the year for me.

ANI: Do you *hear me*? It's hard enough for me to put myself in space when that space is *mine*. I don't go out, I work alone. I design and make —

these — amazing little dresses for little girls — one-of-a-kind little works of art that no one wants to buy this year. So I don't have a lot of contact with other people. I really thought this might be *fun,* try out a few *ideas,* talk about *Socrates!*

MAYANNAH: But this is my yearly ritual: the meat, the blood, the strangers, and the crazy hope I invest.

ANI: But I don't even know what you're celebrating. You never told me.

MAYANNAH: It's hunger. Hunger is why we're here.

ANI: Oh, that's not creepy — or vague!

MAYANNAH: *Mira,* I'll double the offer . . . forty thousand, cash, *tonight . . .* just sit down and eat your dinner.

ANI: Forty? In cash?

MAYANNAH: This isn't going to be like the other years . . . I'm not going to let everything fall apart. I'm not going to scare everyone away. I don't care what it costs me.

ANI: You'd really make it forty?

MAYANNAH: I can do everything better. Just let me start over. Music! *(She goes offstage.)*
(Alone. Ani fights her desire to run away. Music plays: an old bolero. Mayannah reenters.)

MAYANNAH: What kind of hostess *am* I? Letting everything get so morbid. *Life's* what's important tonight. Let's talk about life! Let's talk about love! *(Mayannah holds Ani and they slow dance together.)*

ANI: *(At a loss.)* So — the parents are dead, huh?

MAYANNAH: Yes — but in life they were so in love, you couldn't be in the room when they got, you know, *that way.* In my life my father was a big success in television.

ANI: Television? Really?

MAYANNAH: My papi was seen and loved by millions. But that was before all the news programs had their balls cut off.

ANI: Seen? Your father was on the air?

MAYANNAH: Remember when they used to have international news? He did those. So I was told by *La Doña.* You see, I have *facts* about my parents but no *memories . . .*

ANI: What time was your father on the air?

MAYANNAH: Twice every day.

ANI: At six and eleven?

MAYANNAH: At six and eleven! How did you know?

ANI: Now you're just fucking with me.

MAYANNAH: Were you a fan? But he died before you were born. For sure, if you saw him, though, he would've driven you crazy.

ANI: Stop saying things like that!

MAYANNAH: *(Laughs.)* Made Mami so jealous! La Doña told me that, in Puerto Rico, my parents loved to take long walks along the beach together. They touched each other in shameless ways, right in front of the birds and joggers! La Doña says my parents were obsessed with tigers. She says they read Borges and Kipling to me every night, spoke about tigers in whispers, and understood them in some weird, amazing way. She says my parents died together. In India. They had an accident. I was eight. That's something you don't forget. I just don't know why I forgot so many other things about them. You know how much money I'd pay to remember one thing about my parents that's all mine? That doesn't come to me predigested from a bunch of overpaid freaks who don't give a shit about me?

ANI: I'm sorry, Mayannah, that's sad, and you should see a qualified professional about that, but —

MAYANNAH: *(Looking at Ani's hands.)* God, I love your hands, Ani . . . that was the first thing I noticed about you, the *hands* . . .

ANI: — that your father was on TV doing news at six and eleven freaks me out a bit because the man I was in love with —

MAYANNAH: In photos of Mami . . . her hands are exactly yours. So soft. So white! *La Doña* says Papi was amused by Mami's white skin. He joked that the glare made him blind. So he called her La Blanquita. It's Spanish for "The White Girl."

(These words seem to send a jolt through Ani's system. She pulls away from Mayannah.)

ANI: Can you shut up about this now?

MAYANNAH: I'm sorry . . . I talk about them so much because I didn't know them.

ANI: But "The White Girl" . . . That's *my* nickname . . .

DR. JEKYLL AND MR. HYDE

Jeffrey Hatcher*

Dramatic
Mr. Hyde, late twenties to early fifties
Elizabeth Jelkes, mid- to late twenties

> *Elizabeth is a very pretty, up-from-the-slums woman who has succeeded at bettering herself, but without losing any of her street smarts or toughness. Mr. Hyde, attractive in a savage "bad boy" way, returns to his rooms to find Elizabeth, who has somehow gotten in so she may question him about his attack on her younger sister a week earlier. In the course of the scene, Hyde becomes attracted to Elizabeth, and Elizabeth, despite Hyde's initial unpleasant behavior, becomes equally intrigued with him.*

> *(Inside Mr. Hyde's room. Sudden change of light as the door turns around quickly. Hyde stands at the door, his back pressed against it, as if he's just slammed it shut after his encounter with Utterson. Hyde sees Elizabeth standing in the room.)*

HYDE: What're you doing here? *(Springs to her, grabs her.)* Answer me! What brings you to my rooms?

ELIZABETH: Your name is Hyde?

HYDE: Who said? Tell me!

ELIZABETH: My mother! My mother said this is where you live!

HYDE: Who's your mother?

ELIZABETH: You gave her money! For my sister, she plays in the street, you had an . . . a —

HYDE: We had a run-in.

ELIZABETH: *(Nods.)* . . . You gave her a check.

HYDE: And it was cashed; the bank is prompt in its reports.

ELIZABETH: My mother drank the money.

HYDE: Your mother has her priorities straight. You haven't answered my question. Why do I find you in my rooms?

ELIZABETH: I wanted to see the man who would do such a thing.

HYDE: Trample a child and take a stick to her? You can see that in any house in London.

ELIZABETH: Trample a child and pay for the privilege.

(Hyde looks at her for a long moment. Then he turns away.)

HYDE: Well, you've seen him. Now go.

(Elizabeth keeps her eyes on him. After a beat, she starts to the door, Hyde's voice stops her.)

HYDE: How'd you get in?

ELIZABETH: Your landlord is a man, I'm a woman.

(Hyde grins and turns to her.)

HYDE: Why didn't you come before? The check was cashed a week ago.

ELIZABETH: I don't come back that often.

HYDE: Back?

ELIZABETH: Home. My family's home. I work near Charing Cross.

HYDE: Ohhh. Got on in the world, did we? Gutter girl who learned a trade and got a room above a shop? What are we, a milliner's assistant? Clerk in a sweets emporium? I'd say you were a governess, but you haven't the breeding.

(Elizabeth turns to go. Hyde steps in front of her, blocking her way. Elizabeth tries to sidestep Hyde. He blocks her again. Hyde and Elizabeth are face-to-face.)

HYDE: The girl, your sister, is she well?

ELIZABETH: She's forgotten the encounter already. The only reason anyone remembers the occurrence is because of the cheque.

HYDE: I assure you, I did not pay willingly.

ELIZABETH: Some of the men from the street said they threatened you if you didn't.

HYDE: It was not their threat I feared; I could have killed them each and all. It was a gentleman showed me the error of my ways.

ELIZABETH: Could you not kill him too?

HYDE: Yes, but the police take note when a gentleman gets his. But you . . . If you were found dead on the street tonight, the constable who came across your corpse would as like sell it cheap as blow his whistle. Find yourself on a gurney being cut into bits, a penny a pound.

(Hyde, quick as lightning, pulls on the handle of his cane and unsheathes a blade, attached to the handle. He shoves it against Elizabeth's throat.)

ELIZABETH: AHH!

HYDE: Don't say you're not afraid of me, Elizabeth.

ELIZABETH: I am afraid.

HYDE: Then run.

ELIZABETH: What if the door is locked?

HYDE: Risk it, it's your only chance.

ELIZABETH: Do women always run from you?

HYDE: They never run.

ELIZABETH: Afraid to?

HYDE: Paid not to.

ELIZABETH: What else do you pay your women not to do?

HYDE: Say no.

ELIZABETH: You're sad. You have to frighten women to keep them. You have to pay them not to go.

HYDE: What makes you so brave?

ELIZABETH: You'll never know me well enough to understand.

(Hyde takes that in. He lowers the blade and slips it back into the cane.)

HYDE: The door's not locked.

ELIZABETH: I knew that. You didn't slip the bolt.

(Elizabeth turns to go.)

HYDE: Wait! I'm not always at home when friends come calling here. *(Takes out a card from his pocket, hands it to her.)* They know me at this house. If ever you have need. What's your name?

ELIZABETH: . . . Elizabeth. Elizabeth —

HYDE: *(Stops her.)* No. Tell me more, and I'll know how to find you.

(Elizabeth remains for a moment. Then she opens the door, exits, and shuts the door behind her.)

KILLERS AND OTHER FAMILY

Lucy Thurber

Dramatic
Elizabeth, twenties
Jeff, twenties

> *Elizabeth (Lizzy) lives in Manhattan, where she is working on her dissertation. Her brother, Jeff, has appeared out of the blue with her former boyfriend, Danny, who hurt her when they were a couple. Jeff is in big trouble and needs money. Here, she lashes out at Jeff for bringing Danny along with him.*

ELIZABETH: I can't believe you brought him here, Jeff. You're not even sorry, are you? You don't look sorry. The first time you come to visit me. I've been asking you to come since college —

JEFF: I know.

ELIZABETH: I wanted *you* to come, not Danny. I told you that. I told you if you ever came you were to come alone, or you could bring Mom. I never wanted him to come. I hate him.

JEFF: You don't hate him.

ELIZABETH: I hate him and you know that. I've worked hard not to have this kind of shit in my life, haven't I?

JEFF: Yes, Lizzy, but —

ELIZABETH: I've told you, I'm on deadline.

JEFF: Yes —

ELIZABETH: I've told you on the phone, I've talked to you about how I'm not

JEFF: I know, Lizzy —

ELIZABETH: You know he hurt me, Jeff, he hurt me, and you brought him here

JEFF: Yes, Lizzy, but —

ELIZABETH: I don't know why it's so hard for you to act like you respect me. I'm your sister. You're supposed to look after me —

JEFF: I do look after you —

ELIZABETH: Like when? Like when we were kids? You always let him do whatever he wanted. You call that looking after me? —

JEFF: That was a long time ago, and I don't want to talk about it.

ELIZABETH: No, you never want to talk about that. OK. Let's talk about who paid the rent last month?

JEFF: Give me a break, Lizzy.

ELIZABETH: And did I get a thanks from either you or Mom?

JEFF: Mom thanked you.

ELIZABETH: She did not.

JEFF: She did, she called you.

ELIZABETH: Not to thank me. She called to cry.

JEFF: She's always crying.

ELIZABETH: 'Cause you're never around to help her.

JEFF: You know that's not true. Look —

ELIZABETH: No, you look; we're all she has and you know that. Why can't you stop her from — ?

JEFF: Yeah, us and half the men in town. You always blame me for everything that ever happens. Why don't you blame Mom? She's the one who brings everybody into the house. You think you're the only one who had things happen to them, Lizzy? You never care about that, about what happened to me. You only care about all the things that happened to you —

ELIZABETH: Fuck you, Jeff.

JEFF: I have dreams too . . .

ELIZABETH: What dreams you got, Jeff? Every dream you ever had, you and Danny drink away. You grew up just like Mom. That's something we promised we'd never do. I kept my promise. Why didn't you?
(Pause.)

JEFF: I don't know — Look, Elizabeth, I'm in trouble, that's why I'm here.
(Pause.)

ELIZABETH: What kind of trouble?

JEFF: Big trouble.
(Pause.)

JEFF: I need your help.

ELIZABETH: What kind of help?

JEFF: I need money.

ELIZABETH: Jesus Jeff . . .

JEFF: I'm sorry, I didn't know where else to go. You're the only person I know with money —

ELIZABETH: I don't have money —

JEFF: You have to, you have to —

ELIZABETH: God, what did you do?

JEFF: I can't tell you, I can't . . . I just, I thought I'd go to Mexico. I thought . . . I talked Danny into it. He doesn't know. Don't tell him. He thinks it's all a big party. You know me, can't do anything alone —

ELIZABETH: Jeff —

JEFF: Elizabeth, please. Who else can I ask? It's bad, it's really bad.

ELIZABETH: I've got my leftover student loan money —

JEFF: Great!

ELIZABETH: It's only three thousand —

JEFF: Jesus!

ELIZABETH: No, it's all I have for the rest of the year —

JEFF: What about your roommate?

ELIZABETH: What about her?

JEFF: She always helps you, don't she?

ELIZABETH: Yes, but . . . Jesus, Jeff, what did you do? You can tell me. I'm your sister —

JEFF: Really, I can't. You wouldn't love me anymore.

ELIZABETH: Listen to me, there is nothing you could do, nothing, it doesn't matter, I swear —

JEFF: There is one thing and I'm doing it now. Please don't ask me any more questions. What I need is to sleep. Will you let me sleep? I haven't slept all night. And you'll get the money, right? You'll get it, and then me and Danny will go, and it will be like we were never here. I promise.

ELIZABETH: *(To Jeff, pointing to the bedroom.)* The bed's in there. I need you and Danny gone before Claire comes home from work. She, she doesn't understand things like this.

JEFF: Good for her, right?

ELIZABETH: Yeah.

JEFF: Will you just entertain him while I sleep? You know how restless he gets.

ELIZABETH: Sure . . .

JEFF: Seriously, Lizzy, I need him here when I wake up. Don't let him talk you into any of his shit.

ELIZABETH: Sure, Jeff . . . I'm not a kid anymore —

JEFF: Elizabeth —

ELIZABETH: I won't, OK. It will be fine. Just get some sleep, I'll — Look, I'll make sure everything's —

JEFF: Elizabeth . . . *(He hugs her.)* I love you.

ELIZABETH: I love you too. You're the only brother I got.

KING OF SHADOWS
Roberto Aguirre-Sacasa

Dramatic
Sarah, teens
Nihar, teens

> *Nihar is a possibly disturbed runaway who claims to have escaped from the Realm of Shadows and to be on the run from the King of Shadows and his consort the Green Lady, who are trying to catch him and bring him back. Strange meteorological things are occurring, and Nihar can predict them before they happen. Sarah lives with her older sister, a social worker who has brought them from the Midwest to San Francisco after both their parents were killed in a helicopter accident. She is a very unhappy girl, and she has bonded with Nihar, who has asked her sister for a place to stay for the night, safe from his "pursuers." Sarah believes Nihar's story.*

(Sarah is carrying a blanket and pillows; there are unpacked cardboard boxes on the floor around them.)

SARAH: Jess keeps saying she's gonna organize; she's gonna turn this extra room into an office for her and Eric, and I'm the only one asking the *obvious* question, which is: Why does a policeman even *need* a home office?

NIHAR: That cop — he, like, *lives* here with you guys?

SARAH: Technically, no. But he pretty much spends every night here — and he showers here — and he eats *here* — and — *(Holding out the blanket and pillows.)* — here, take these *linens* and I'll get the air mattress —

NIHAR: Oh, no, that's OK — *(He takes the stuff from her.)* — the floor's fine.

SARAH: Yeah, but it's one of those self-inflating, state-of-the-art air-mattresses with, you know, adjustable firmness, and —

NIHAR: No, seriously, this is — I would prefer this, actually.

(He kneels down, starts spreading out the blanket, getting settled.)

SARAH: OK, well . . . If you need anything . . .

NIHAR: I think I'm good.

SARAH: OK, well. Um . . . *(She smiles at him. It is a very wan smile.)*

NIHAR: What?

SARAH: That . . . Kingdom of Shadows place? I don't think I've ever *been* to it, per se, but your pictures, your drawings reminded me . . . *(Beat.)* We were at our parents' funeral, Jess and I, we were standing on this hill, at the cemetery, and . . . I wasn't sad at all, or I guess it hadn't affected me yet or whatever . . . And the priest was eulogizing, and I looked over to where there were these trees, this grove of trees, moving in the wind, and . . .

NIHAR: *Here — (He clears a space for her on his blanket.)* you can sit, if you want.

SARAH: Thanks, I — *(She sits next to him)* Next to the trees, under the, like, canopy of leaves, there was this . . . beautiful woman, standing there, waving at me. And at first I thought it was my mom, but then I was like, no, no, she's dead, and then I thought it was my guardian angel, or a ghost, except she was . . . Nihar, I'm not even lying, but I think she was green . . . Her skin, her hair, everything . . . And she was, like, *beckoning* for me to follow her — and I think maybe I even started walking towards her . . . But then Jess grabbed my hand — and pulled me close — and I refocused on what the priest was saying . . . And when I looked back, the woman wasn't there, and the trees weren't waving to me anymore, and *then* . . . *that's* when I got sad. *(Short pause.)* Is it crazy that I just remembered that?

NIHAR: That was her — the Green Lady — that was absolutely, *absolutely* her.

SARAH: Nihar . . .

NIHAR: What?

SARAH: . . . I like girls, OK?

NIHAR: Yeah . . . ?

SARAH: . . . and though we've been having issues (like, for instance, she's always playing mind games with me), I have a pretty serious girlfriend . . .

NIHAR: OK . . .

SARAH: . . . and I know you're gay (though I doubt you have a boyfriend 'cause of your transient lifestyle) . . .

NIHAR: Yeah, I'm pretty much only sleeping with guys professionally these days.

SARAH: . . . but if we don't kiss right now . . . right this second —

NIHAR: — I agree.

SARAH: Really? Are you — you're sure?

(Nihar takes Sarah's face in his hands, and the two kids lean in and kiss . . . and kiss . . .)

A LIGHT LUNCH
A. R. Gurney

Comic
Beth, thirties
Viola, twenties

>   *Beth, a young attorney from Texas, has arrived at a restaurant in the*
>   *New York City theater district for a power lunch with the playwright*
>   *A. R. Gurney's agent, who hasn't arrived yet. She represents a Texas ty-*
>   *coon who wants to option Gurney's latest play. The tycoon hasn't read*
>   *the play, but he knows it's about President George W. Bush. Viola, an*
>   *aspiring actor, is Beth's waitress.*

>   *(Beth enters briskly. She is wearing a stylish suit and carrying a classy brief-*
>   *case. She is followed by Viola, wearing an apron and holding a couple of*
>   *well-used menus).*

BETH: *(Surveying the area.)* This will do.

VIOLA: You asked to be off in a corner.

BETH: We don't want to disturb other people.

VIOLA: And you don't want other people to disturb you.

BETH: Exactly.

VIOLA: May I ask . . . will this be a . . . well, a romantic meeting?

BETH: Oh no, no, no, no.

VIOLA: I could easily put fresh flowers on the table.

BETH: Don't bother. This is strictly a working lunch. All business, from the
get-go.

VIOLA: Gotcha. *(Distributing menus.)* I'm Viola, by the way. I'll be serving you
today.

BETH: Hi, Viola. *(Looking off.)* Will there be people at those tables nearby?

VIOLA: Not these days.

BETH: Why not these days?

VIOLA: The recession and all.

BETH: Oh that.

VIOLA: More and more people are settling for sandwiches at their desks.
If they still have desks.

BETH: Yes, well, the reason I'm being a stickler is that we'll probably be tossing some familiar names around the infield, and I don't want strangers listening in.

VIOLA: Are you in the theater?

BETH: No, no. I'm just a lowly lawyer. But I'll be meeting with a theater person. About theater things. He recommended this restaurant.

VIOLA: That's because theater people come here all the time. Lauren Bacall ate a mushroom omelet here. Alec Baldwin sat at this very table.

BETH: Oh well. We're hardly in that category.

VIOLA: I'm in show business myself.

BETH: Are you really?

VIOLA: Oh yes. I act. I wait to act. Get it?

BETH: I do. And your name is, again?

VIOLA: Viola.

BETH: Viola's a pretty name.

VIOLA: I took it from the character in *Twelfth Night*. I played her in high school.

BETH: Interesting.

VIOLA: My real name is Mildred, but I don't broadcast it. In high school they called me Mildewed.

BETH: Oh dear.

VIOLA: You can see why I had to change it.

BETH: I do, I do.

VIOLA: *(Reciting.)* "I prithee, and I'll pay thee bounteously, Conceal me what I am, and be my aid . . ."

BETH: I won't tell a soul, Viola. But since you're an actress . . .

VIOLA: Actor. Actresses are actors now.

BETH: All right. Since you're an actor, may I ask a quick question about the theater?

VIOLA: Go ahead.

BETH: Have you ever heard of a playwright named Gurney?

VIOLA: Who?

BETH: Gurney.

VIOLA: Now wait. I'm thinking. I believe my boyfriend knows more about him. He teaches theater.

BETH: Gurney?

VIOLA: No, my boyfriend.

BETH: What does he say about Gurney?

VIOLA: Let's see. Gurney. Hmmm. Is he the one who's been around, like, forever?

BETH: I believe so. Yes.

VIOLA: And he writes plays about Wasps?

BETH: Apparently, yes.

VIOLA: But not just Wasps. I think my boyfriend said that some of Gurney's plays now have Jewish people in them.

BETH: I should hope so.

VIOLA: Is Gurney the person you're meeting with today?

BETH: Good God no. Just with his agent.

VIOLA: His agent? Oh hey! Does his agent handle actors?

BETH: That I wouldn't know.

VIOLA: Would you mind if I slipped my headshot and résumé into his dessert menu?

BETH: Up to you.

VIOLA: As Shakespeare says in *Twelfth Night*, "Some are born great, some achieve greatness, but agents have greatness thrust upon them."

BETH: Very good, Viola. *(Glancing off.)* It's hard to see the door from here. Will you be keeping an eye out for him?

VIOLA: Oh sure. I'll do it now.

    (Starts off.)

BETH: I have no idea what he looks like. We've only talked on the telephone.

VIOLA: No problem. I can spot an agent a mile away.

PERFECT HARMONY
Andrew Grosso and The Essentials

Comic
Valerie, fifteen
Simon, fourteen

Valerie Smooter is a member of her high school's girls' a cappella group, the Ladies in Red. She sings with perfect pitch. Valerie has a fear of being looked at, and last year she panicked at the nationals and refused to go onstage. She's been working on her phobia this year, but as the nationals get closer, the pressure is increasing. Simon Depardieu is an angel-voiced freshman in The Acafellas, the school's boys' a cappella group. Simon suffers from temporomandibular joint disorder (inflammation of the jaw joint) and severe canker sores; both ailments are exacerbated by stress. When The Acafellas' collective urine sample at the regionals tested positive for estrogen, all eyes turned toward him — but Simon insists he's innocent. Simon and Valerie, the two young, oddball introverts in their highly competitive performance groups, have found each other and struck up a quiet, secret friendship. Or is it more than that . . .

(Crossfade to Simon and Valerie comparing notes.)

VALERIE: It hasn't gotten easier, it's gotten worse. Don't look at me. I keep looking out, and I keep seeing them all looking right back on stage. Even when I don't look out, I know they're all looking at me. And now nationals are on TV. TV! Don't look at me.

SIMON: Maybe you can stand behind Megan when she's moving side to side.

VALERIE: I tried that — don't look at me — but she keeps moving so much, I kept being exposed.

SIMON: What if you sang behind a screen, and everyone else stood in front?

VALERIE: We already tried that, Melody said that was too distracting.

SIMON: Maybe if the —

VALERIE: Don't look at me.

SIMON: — audience could close their eyes.

VALERIE: Half of them would cheat and still see me. Don't look at me. Meghan said that God's watching me too. All the time.

SIMON: My mom said that once. I think it's nice.

VALERIE: It's not nice, it's — don't look at me — I'm not — I've got to do something. What do you do when you get so nervous?

SIMON: Valium's good, and cortisone injections really help to relax everything.

VALERIE: Wow. You do, do drugs.

SIMON: Ever since I was little. But not since I joined the group. It's so hard to have this gift of song and then not to be able to use it because I can't open my mouth.

VALERIE: You do have nice pitch.

SIMON: Thanks, you have great pitch.

VALERIE: I know. I sound perfect.

SIMON: I really want to look at you.

VALERIE: I know.

SIMON: Why can't I look at you?

VALERIE: You just can't. No one can.

SIMON: Why?

VALERIE: I just don't like to be seen.

SIMON: Why don't you skip nationals then?

VALERIE: I promised the girls I'd sing with them. — You're looking at me.

SIMON: I know.

VALERIE: Wow.

SIMON: I know.

VALERIE: I know.

SIMON: You could try a burka.

VALERIE: Those are really demeaning. Don't look at me. I do wish I could be totally covered. There'd be so much less to look at.

SIMON: Maybe you could find something that's like a burka but not so demeaning — like a wetsuit.

UNDER THE POMEGRANATE TREES
Don Nigro

Seriocomic
Patty, nineteen
Sharon, nineteen

> *Coeds Patty and Sharon are sitting on lawn chairs in the backyard of an apartment near the campus of Arizona State University in Tempe in the autumn of 1968. They're wearing swimsuits and drinking beer. It's night, but we can see them by moonlight. Patty is blonde, Sharon brunette. All the boys have always wanted Patty. This is the source of considerable tension in their relationship, which most of the time remains under the surface, but more and more it's starting to bubble out. This scene is the beginning of what will later become a serious point of contention between them.*

PATTY: It's finally cooling off a little bit. I had too much sun. This is not the climate for me. I burn easily. I'm highly combustible.

SHARON: You've got to be more careful.

PATTY: I'm not careful. That's my trademark. I could spontaneously combust at any moment.

SHARON: You're extremely fair skinned.

PATTY: You're lucky. You tan, and I go all lobstery. I envy brunettes. I really do.

SHARON: No you don't.

PATTY: OK, I don't. Well, sometimes I do. I get tired of being looked at.

SHARON: No you don't.

PATTY: You know what? You and I have known each other way too long.

SHARON: This is true.

PATTY: I was thinking about the pomegranate trees. Do you remember?

SHARON: I remember.

PATTY: How cool it was there? That long row of them, with the dirt pathway underneath, by the playing fields?

SHARON: It was nice there.

PATTY: I loved it there.

SHARON: It was really nice.

PATTY: What was that girl's name?

SHARON: Which girl? There were a lot of girls.

PATTY: The one who used to pull her dress up. She used to pull her dress up for the boys.

SHARON: I don't remember that.

PATTY: Yes you do. She liked to tease them. She was a tease. She'd show them more and more. Right in front of everybody.

SHARON: Cindy.

PATTY: Was it Cindy? The one with the horse?

SHARON: Shelley had the horse.

PATTY: Then it was Cindy.

SHARON: I wonder what happened to her.

PATTY: She's probably on drugs.

SHARON: Everybody's on drugs.

PATTY: I don't mean casually. I mean seriously on drugs. Cindy was one messed-up puppy.

SHARON: She was really smart.

PATTY: She was very smart, but she was totally messed up. Probably at home. Some sort of molestation in that family.

SHARON: You think so?

PATTY: Why else would she do that?

SHARON: Maybe she just liked to lift up her skirt for boys. Maybe it was a power thing.

PATTY: I don't think so.

SHARON: You were swimming naked with some of those same boys last summer.

PATTY: So? What's your point?

SHARON: My point is, what's the difference?

PATTY: There's a lot of difference.

SHARON: What is it?

PATTY: Well, we were just swimming.

SHARON: You were completely naked, Patty.

PATTY: Yes, but we were swimming.

SHARON: But you liked it, didn't you?

PATTY: I like swimming.

SHARON: You liked when they looked at you. You liked it that they all wanted you.

PATTY: I was pretending I was Marilyn. You know. Swimming naked in that last movie they never finished because she died?

SHARON: Now there's a great role model for you.

PATTY: Marilyn was very smart.

SHARON: She was on drugs, too.

PATTY: I heard she was murdered.

SHARON: I don't think so.

PATTY: You think she killed herself?

SHARON: No, I think the doctors killed her.

PATTY: Why would her doctors kill her?

SHARON: Because they're doctors. They take an oath. Don't let anybody get out of here alive. That's what doctors are for. To keep the population down. Plus they were men.

PATTY: So?

SHARON: Men worship beauty, but they also want to kill it because they fear it, because of its power to enslave them.

PATTY: That's kind of dark, Sharon.

SHARON: I'm a dark girl. I tan. You burn.

PATTY: You've thought about this a lot, haven't you?

SHARON: More than you.

PATTY: You're turning into a very bitter little person.

SHARON: I'm not turning into anything.

THE WAR PARTY
Vincent Delaney

Dramatic
Laura Smith, fifty
Jessie, early twenties

> *On the night of her failed reelection bid, Laura Smith, a right-wing senator, is confronted by Jessie, a young intern and campaign volunteer who's not what she seems. As they work their way through three bottles of champagne, the gloves come off, and two tough, political women fight for survival.*

LAURA: *(Sweet.)* So, Jessie, tell me about telemarketing.

JESSIE: Telemarketing.

LAURA: I mean outreach. I'm curious.

JESSIE: Maybe I should go.

LAURA: No, no. Sit. How does it work?

JESSIE: Well, we get the lists — the names —

LAURA: From where?

JESSIE: They buy them actually, there are companies —

LAURA: So then what?

JESSIE: You know, maybe I should —

LAURA: Then what?

JESSIE: Well, I'm there with a headset, and I've got the person's name on my screen —

LAURA: That's it? Just the name?

JESSIE: No, they give us other information.

LAURA: Like what?

JESSIE: Well, just stuff to work with. Cold calling is tough.

LAURA: Like?

JESSIE: Well, income —

LAURA: You know their incomes?

JESSIE: Well, yeah. We have to know what they make.

LAURA: You don't call the poor folk.

JESSIE: Waste of time.

LAURA: What else?

JESSIE: Hobbies, race —

LAURA: Race?

JESSIE: We don't care about it. I don't say, hi Mr. Rubeo. I see here you're Hispanic, so who are you voting for?

LAURA: So what do you say?

JESSIE: Hi, I'm Jessie, calling on behalf of Senator Smith. Is this Mr. Rubeo?

LAURA: *(Bad accent.)* Si, senorita.

JESSIE: Super. How are you doing this evening?

LAURA: Muy bien.

JESSIE: I see here you're Hispanic. That's a joke, Laura. I'm calling to talk about Senator Smith.

LAURA: Hurry up, my kids are screaming; I have seven.

JESSIE: Laura, that's a stereotype!

LAURA: I have seven kids!

JESSIE: OK, well, Senator Smith fights for education.

LAURA: Then why can't my kids read?

JESSIE: We're very concerned. Senator Smith believes —

LAURA: I was joking, my kids are scholars.

JESSIE: You have a fine sense of humor, Mr. Rubeo. Have you considered a contribution?

LAURA: My wife would kill me, she's a Democrat.

JESSIE: We don't have to tell her, do we? It'll be our secret.

LAURA: You have a sexy voice. What did you say your name was?

JESSIE: Jessie. You sound special, too.

LAURA: How old are you?

JESSIE: You'll have to pay for that information.

LAURA: *(Breaking the role-play.)* You really are quite good at this, aren't you?

JESSIE: Hours of practice. I had one crotchety old biddy, wouldn't let me say a word. Just went on and on how she hadn't voted since Kennedy, and since she hadn't gotten the full four years out of him, she wasn't about to vote again. And I'm just, uh-huh, I see, oh my, for five minutes. Then she announces I've changed her life, and how much would we like?

LAURA: What did you say?

JESSIE: Fifteen thousand. On her credit card. Right then and there.

LAURA: Fifteen thousand?

JESSIE: Well, come on, we needed it.

LAURA: That's against the law.

JESSIE: We do it all the time.

LAURA: You broke the law?

JESSIE: Well, your campaign did. I didn't personally.

LAURA: What's the worst thing they say to you?

JESSIE: Oh, you don't want to —

LAURA: Sure I do. Tell me.

JESSIE: People get grouchy sometimes, after dinner, you know —

LAURA: Let's hear it.

JESSIE: Well, they swear sometimes —

LAURA: Like what?

JESSIE: Oh, fuck you, fuck you bitch, fuck you you fucking bitch, stuff like that.

LAURA: Really? What did they say about me?

JESSIE: Laura, ninety-nine percent of the people I called were gracious —

LAURA: Tell me —

JESSIE: Receptive —

LAURA: Tell me —

JESSIE: Thoughtful —

LAURA: TELL ME, TELL ME, TELL ME, what did they say about me!

JESSIE: That right-wing racist homophobic helmet-headed bitch will never get a cent out of me! Could I have some more champagne?

WHAT TO DO WHEN YOU HATE ALL YOUR FRIENDS
Larry Kunofsky

Comic
Enid, midtwenties to early thirties
Holly, midtwenties to early thirties

> *Enid, our narrator, clues us in on the secret goings-on of The Friends,*
> *a secret friendship society with elaborate rules and an intricate ranking*
> *system. Enid is not a member of The Friends. She is a lowercase-F*
> *friend. Everyone assures her that The Friends is no big deal, and yet it*
> *does seem to be a very big deal to Holly. She is about the same age as*
> *Enid and is a former member-in-good-standing of The Friends, but*
> *now, on the night of her birthday party, she seems to be dealing with a*
> *low ranking within the group.*

ENID: *(To audience.)* I've been invited to so many parties lately. I feel like the
most popular of peripheral lowercase friends. The party tonight is really
special because it's a special birthday for Holly.
*(Holly enters. She's really unhappy. She heads for the liquor cabinet. She's
drunk, but is trying to hold it together.)*

ENID: *(Continued.)* And everyone was really happy and really excited to be
celebrating with her. This is a really happy day for her.

HOLLY: Enid, maybe don't say anything for a while.

ENID: Happy birthday, Holly.

HOLLY: Enid. Seriously. You don't have to say that every time I fix myself another drink.

ENID: *(To audience.)* I can't help it. I'm just so happy for Holly. I mean, I can
relate. It's my birthday, too. And that makes me especially happy to see
Holly receive the recognition she deserves. I mean, this isn't Holly's *ac-
tual* birthday. You get to have three birthday parties throughout the year
when you're a capital-F friend.

HOLLY: Enid, no one knows what you're talking about. There's nothing special going on here! Nothing special at all.

ENID: *(To audience.)* This was Holly's second special birthday party this year. The first party was really special. There were celebrity guests. And the secret hot tub that only a few people know about.

HOLLY: There's no hot tub, Enid.

ENID: *(To audience.)* But this second birthday party . . . well . . . the evening's still young.

(Holly snaps a little bit at this. But, instead of lashing out at Enid, she lashes out at us.)

HOLLY: *(To audience.)* I saw that. I saw that look! I can tell that you're judging us.

ENID: Holly.

HOLLY: *(To audience.)* How. Dare. You.

ENID: Holly, maybe you shouldn't.

HOLLY: *(To audience.)* Who do you think you are?! You think friends is easy?! What? You've never been let down by a friend? You've never let a friend down yourself? If you think that, then you're just lying to yourself, buddy boy!

ENID: Holly.

HOLLY: What's wrong, Enid? Think you're the only on who can "narrate"? Well check it, Enid, I've got me some mad narrating skills, how'd ya like them apples?!

ENID: Holly. When you narrate . . . it's nice to . . . just be nice.

HOLLY: Everything's nice to you, Enid!

ENID: It's nice to have people rooting for you. It's nice to have people on your side. Y'know?

(Holly turns to us. She takes a good long look at us. She wants us to like her. She really does.)

HOLLY: Yeah. I do know. *(To audience again.)* Thank you for dressing so elegantly and being so attractive in general and everything.

ENID: *(To audience.)* Holly was going through a rough time.

HOLLY: What are you talking about?! What rough time?! This is smooth sailing for me. Life's a frikking breeze!

ENID: OK. *(To audience.)* But Holly was going through a really rough time!

HOLLY: Are you saying that I'm drunk? Because if you're saying I'm drunk, Enid, then the rough time is the time that your face will be having with my open fists.

ENID: Uh. Happy birthday?

WHERE WE'RE BORN
Lucy Thurber

Dramatic
Lilly, twenties
Franky, twenties

> *Lilly is a college student on spring break. She is staying with her cousin,*
> *Tony, who she has always viewed as her protector because she is es-*
> *tranged form her mother. Franky, Tony's girlfriend, is a waitress. She is*
> *very pretty and exudes a smart toughness. Lilly is attracted to Franky,*
> *and in this scene, she does something about it.*

LILLY: You OK?

FRANKY: Fine.

LILLY: Good . . . Tony passed out on the couch.

FRANKY: Yeah.

LILLY: So . . . can I sleep in here tonight?

FRANKY: Sure.

LILLY: *(She crosses to the bed and sits down. She reaches for Franky's hand.)*
I'm pretty drunk. I'm sorry.

FRANKY: I'm drunk too.

LILLY: No. I'm sorry about Tony.

FRANKY: *(She withdraws her hand.)* Me too.

LILLY: *(She takes her hand again.)* He just likes to show off. I had fun dancing
at least. Did you?

FRANKY: Yeah . . .

LILLY: Yeah, funny. I wanted to hurt him when he touched you like that. I
don't like it when he's like that. Every time I see him it's like he's farther
away. He never used to do stuff like that, or did he? I guess he did. I always used to be able to talk to Tony. Didn't I? Like today he came and
got me when nobody else would. He knew I wanted to come home. He
always knows things about me. Doesn't he?

FRANKY: I guess.

LILLY: Am I boring you?

FRANKY: Lilly, it's just that —

LILLY: I don't mean to bore you.

FRANKY: I can't fix it for you, Lilly.

LILLY: Fix what?

FRANKY: Whatever you got that needs fixing. I can't fix anything. I just go around and around.

LILLY: 'Cause he hit you?

FRANKY: No.

LILLY: Because he makes you lonely?

FRANKY: In a way, I guess. Or maybe, it's 'cause in the end everything's lonely. Lilly, what are you doing?

LILLY: I don't know. *(Lilly kisses her. Franky kisses her back and then pushes her away.)*

FRANKY: Whoa, whoa! What the fuck was that?!

LILLY: God, that felt good, didn't it? God that felt so — Shit, I want to — You're so beautiful . . . *(Touching her.)*

FRANKY: Lilly, you're really drunk. Why don't we just go to sleep? Come on, Lilly, you're really drunk. Why don't we just go to sleep? Come on, Lilly, lay down. *(She gently pushes Lilly down on the bed. Lilly grabs her and pulls her down with her onto the bed. Lilly kisses Franky's neck, lying under her.)* Oh shit, Lilly, whoa, whoa, take it easy. You're drunk, OK? Sometimes when people are drunk, you know, shit like this happens. We're just gonna go to sleep and every thing will be fine in the morning.

LILLY: *(Letting go of her.)* You don't like me.

FRANKY: *(Getting off her.)* Sure I like you, Lill. I like you a lot. It's just time for bed, that's all.

LILLY: No, you don't like me as much as I like you!

FRANKY: Shit. Lilly, I love you . . .

LILLY: You don't, you don't!

FRANKY: *(Patting Lilly's shoulder.)* Hey, come on Lilly, it's time for sleep.

LILLY: *(Sitting up and seeming suddenly sober.)* Please, please I want to so badly. I can't stand how bad I want to. You want to too, don't you? *(Lilly leans toward Franky. Taking her face in both hands, she kisses her. Lilly pushes Franky back onto the bed, lying on top of her. Franky's arms come around Lilly as they kiss. Lilly kisses Franky's neck. Franky suddenly pushes Lilly off her. She jumps off the bed and back toward the door. The women stare at each other. Franky reaches the bedroom door.)*

FRANKY: I'm going out to sleep with Tony. You can have the bed.

LILLY: Great, thanks.

FRANKY: Well, OK, sleep well. *(She hesitates by the door, looking at Lilly.)*

LILLY: Please don't go.

FRANKY: I . . . Jesus, Lilly, Jesus! I don't know. I gotta get out of here. *(Franky opens the bedroom door and stands in the doorway. She looks out at Tony on the couch and then back to Lilly. The women look at each other. There is a pause. Franky walks back into the bedroom, closing the door behind her. Lilly looks away.)* Lilly.

LILLY: What?

FRANKY: Look at me.

LILLY: Why?

FRANKY: Because I asked you to. *(Lilly looks at Franky.)* You're a good-looking kid, Lilly.

LILLY: Yeah? What's the operative word there, good-looking or kid?

FRANKY: Good-looking is two words, isn't it? So is this what you've been doing at college?

LILLY: What?

FRANKY: You been kissing all the girls?

LILLY: No.

FRANKY: No? You sure?

LILLY: Yes, I'm fuckin' sure! What the hell are you still doing in here? Go out to Tony!

FRANKY: Keep your voice down.

LILLY: No!

FRANKY: You asked me not to leave and I didn't. Now I'm asking you to keep your voice down. Do you think you can do that?

LILLY: Yes.

FRANKY: Good. So am I the first girl you ever kissed? Answer me: Am I the first?

LILLY: Yes.

FRANKY: Good. I always wanted to be the first at something.

LILLY: What the fuck does that mean?

(Franky crosses to her, pushes her down on the bed, and starts kissing her. Lilly pulls away.)

LILLY: OK, OK.

FRANKY: No, come back, don't stop.

LILLY: Franky, I can't.

FRANKY: Sure you can. You just were.

LILLY: I'm scared.

FRANKY: You're scared? What are you scared of?

LILLY: You.

FRANKY: Me? Nobody's ever been afraid of me in my whole life. What do you got to be afraid of?

LILLY: What you're doing to me.

FRANKY: Yeah? What 'bout what you're doing to me? Maybe you're scared of that? What you gonna do to me, Lilly? *(She touches Lilly.)*

LILLY: *(Pulling away.)* Don't.

FRANKY: Oh come on. What did you think? You think no one was ever gonna say yes to you? Well, I'm saying it. I'm the one that said it. You wanna know? I'm the one who's gonna show you. 'Cause I'm the one who likes the way you feel. *(She pushes Lilly back down on the bed and begins to make love to her. Lights fade down.)*

Rights and Permissions

The complete text of every play in this volumn is available from the performance rights holder, except as otherwise noted.

Note: **For playwrights whose names are followed by an asterisk (*), information can be found about them on the "Meet Our Authors" web page at www.smithandkraus.com.**

MONOLOGUES

ALIENS WITH EXTRAORDINARY SKILLS © 2008 by Saviana Stanescu.* Reprinted by permission of the author. For performance rights, contact Samuel French, Inc. (www.samuelfrench.com) (212-206-8990).

ALOHA SAY THE PRETTY GIRLS © 2007 by Naomi Iizuka. Reprinted by permission of Morgan Jenness, Abrams Artists Agency. For performance rights, contact Playscripts, Inc., 450 7th Ave. #803, New York, NY 10123 (www.playscripts.com) (866-639-7529).

AMERICAN GIRLS © 2008 Hillary Bettis.* Reprinted by permission of the author. For performance rights, contact the author (hbettis05@gmail .com).

AMERICAN HWANGAP © 2008 by Lloyd Suh. Reprinted by permission of Beth Blickers, Abrams Artists Agency. For performance rights, contact Beth Blickers (beth.blickers@abramsartny.com).

AMERICAN MAGIC © 2008 by Gil Kofman.* Reprinted by permission of the author. For performance rights, contact Broadway Play Publishing, 56 E. 81st St., New York, NY 10021 (www.broadwayplaypubl.com) (212-772-8334).

AMERICAN SLIGO © 2008 by Adam Rapp. Reprinted by permission of Farrar, Straus & Giroux LLC. For performance rights, contact Broadway Play Publishing, 56 E. 81st St., New York, NY 10021 (www.broadway-playpubl.com) (212-772-8334).

ANIMALS OUT OF PAPER © 2008 by Rajiv Joseph. Reprinted by permission of Seth Glewen, The Gersh Agency. For performance rights, contact Dramatists Play Service, 440 Park Ave. S., New York, NY 10016 (www.dramatists.com) (212-683-8960).

BAGGAGE © 2008 Sam Bobrick.* Reprinted by permission of the author. For performance rights, contact Samuel French, Inc. (www.samuel french.com) (212-206-8990).

SCENES